DECLUTTER WC
Illustrated DIY Projects i
LUIGI HARBIN

Text Copyright © Luigi Harbin

All rights reserved. No part of this guide may be reproduced in any form without permission in writing from the publisher except in the case of brief quotations embodied in critical articles or reviews.

Legal & Disclaimer

The information contained in this book and its contents is not designed to replace or take the place of any form of medical or professional advice; and is not meant to replace the need for independent medical, financial, legal or other professional advice or services, as may be required. The content and information in this book have been provided for educational and entertainment purposes only.

The content and information contained in this book has been compiled from sources deemed reliable, and it is accurate to the best of the Author's knowledge, information and belief. However, the Author cannot guarantee its accuracy and validity and cannot be held liable for any errors and/or omissions. Further, changes are periodically made to this book as and when needed. Where appropriate and/or necessary, you must consult a professional (including but not limited to your doctor, attorney, financial advisor or such other professional advisor) before using any of the suggested remedies, techniques, or information in this book.

Upon using the contents and information contained in this book, you agree to hold harmless the Author from and against any damages, costs, and expenses, including any legal fees potentially resulting from the application of any of the information provided by this book. This disclaimer applies to any loss, damages or injury caused by the use and application, whether directly or indirectly, of any advice or information presented, whether for breach of contract, tort, negligence, personal injury, criminal intent, or under any other cause of action.

You agree to accept all risks of using the information presented inside this book.

You agree that by continuing to read this book, where appropriate and/or necessary, you shall consult a professional (including but not limited to your doctor, attorney, or financial advisor or such other advisor as needed) before using any of the suggested remedies, techniques, or information in this book.

Table of Contents

Introduction - Cleaning Less in a Cleaner Home 6
Chapter 1 - Where Do I Start? 7

    The Wonderful Benefits of Decluttering.. 7
    Avoiding Overwhelming Feelings 9
    Breaking Bad Habits 10
    Why You Need a Cleaning Routine 10
    DIY Projects vs. Store-Bought Products for Decluttering 11

Chapter 2 - Starting Small 14

    Simple Cleaning Must-Haves 14
    Daily, Weekly, Monthly, and Seasonal Cleaning Tasks 15
    Monthly and Seasonal Tasks 17

Chapter 3 – How to Start Decluttering 19

    Bathrooms 20
    Living Spaces 21
    Bedrooms 22
    Kitchen 24
    Garage 26
    Miscellaneous 27
    What to Do with Your Clutter 28

Chapter 4 – DIY Projects for the Home 29
Chapter 5 - DIY Projects for Decluttering your Bathroom 32
Chapter 6 - DIY Projects for Decluttering your Living Space 74
Chapter 7 - DIY Projects for Decluttering your Bedroom 85

    Stuffed Toy Zoo 133

Chapter 8 - DIY Projects for Decluttering your Kitchen 174
Chapter 9 - DIY Projects for De-cluttering your Garage 249
Chapter 10 - DIY Projects for Decluttering Your Home Office 305
Chapter 11 - Turning Method into Habit 311
Conclusion 312
Check Out Other Books 314

Introduction - Cleaning Less in a Cleaner Home

It is easy to dream of having a spotless home. One with clean floors, a scented bathroom, a gleaming kitchen, and a tidy organised bedroom. The means of achieving this, the actual cleaning, is something we choose not to think about.

A cleaning schedule is almost impossible to follow. Other priorities get in the way. Sounds familiar? Homekeeping is actually a learned behavior. Learning how to do this well will bring in harmony and a peace of mind.

Live stress-free and keep anxiety at bay when it comes to keeping things in order. Your time is now.

Chapter 1 - Where Do I Start?

The Wonderful Benefits of Decluttering

Clutter is defined as a "collection of things, lying about in an untidy mess". How exactly does it form? How does a neatly stacked albums end up being clutter?

Basically, clutter forms when one loses control. When someone fails to make a decision, things have the tendency to pile up and clutter. Eventually, the pile becomes too overwhelming to tackle, and you are overcome by the mess you failed to put aside.

Finding some order and conquering your clutter helps to get rid of the mess. Decluttering, however, is fairly specific in intent. Basically, it is keeping things in order and in their rightful place. It also involves removing things that no longer belong in your home (or your life), because they waste not only your space, but your time and energy as well.

Okay let's make things simple—decluttering is good because of the following reasons:

1. It saves you a lot of time. The simplest benefit to living a clutter-free life is being able to avoid obstacles that only cause time delay. When your house is messy, you end up spending extra minutes trying to locate anything in your home. However, when things are organized in their respective places, you

navigate through your house more conveniently, and time that is precious is significantly maximized.

2. It can reduce anxiety. A messy environment creates unwanted chaos in the mind. Clutter brings unnecessary stimuli that you would rather do without. But when you are able to deal with it, you will notice that your stress and anxiety is significantly reduced—and life is more peaceful.

3. It can give you better sleep. It's never easy to find restful sleep when you have so many things going on in your head. During sleep, after your close your eyes and your physical body is resting, your mental activity is not completely shut down. As a matter of fact, the brain is continuously scanning for danger or navigating through the different external stimuli. The mess in your bedroom will most likely invade the serenity of your sleep, so keeping all kinds of "triggers" away will allow your brain to succumb to absolute rest.

4. It improves your creativity and productivity. Distraction gets in the way of one's smooth and productive thinking. When your mind is cluttered with distractions, it is more difficult to brainstorm. But when your mind is free, the liberation permits free range to exercise one's creativity. In the end, you are more productive and successful.

5. It simplifies your life. After a massive decluttering, you will be left with fewer possessions than when you started. This journey will force you to rethink your priorities. If you didn't pay

attention before, you will be more aware now. You will realize that you actually need less things, so you will no longer struggle with impulse buys. Decluttering keeps things in perspective—and teaches you to live simply.

6. Your house is going to be so much cleaner. This is, of course, the most obvious benefit to decluttering. Everything is organized, so your house is clean, and there is a higher chance that it is allergen-free and disease-free. A clean home is a healthy home—apart from this, it will look so much better.

7. Not just for aesthetic appeal, you work on decluttering your physical space because it has amazing health benefits. If you are still unconvinced, this book is going to give you hundreds of ideas that will surely open your mind. And its effect goes even beyond, because keeping things in perfect order, ultimately improves human relations within the home. When things are clean and orderly, stress is reduced and this eventually translates to harmony.

Avoiding Overwhelming Feelings

The unsurmountable tasks ahead of you are daunting. The good news is you are not alone. Not everyone has their life all put together in a pretty bow. There is work that needs doing, but the results will be worth it. Keep in mind that if you dedicate yourself to de-cluttering your home, you must do your part.

Cleaning up doesn't have to be a chore as well. It is easy to think that it is, but the secret is establishing a more welcoming, positive mindset in order for you to thoroughly enjoy and feel the satisfaction once you've done your daily tasks. Focus is essential to cleaning and it helps you stay on your goals and work on them.

Breaking Bad Habits

There is no question that a well-established cleaning routine goes a long way. Fight the battle one day at a time. You don't have to clean the whole house in one day. that would suck the time and energy out of you, leaving you to dread the next general cleaning day ahead. Instead, develop a schedule that allows you to take only a few minutes of the day to clean a specific area. Then the next day, use those 10 minutes to clean another area of the house. Breaking tasks into smaller chores saves your energy. Focus on a specific area for the week. In the long run, you will end up with a cleaner house. And it will seem less daunting.

It will be difficult to commit yourself to a whole day of cleaning per week. Effectiveness is the key to reaching your goal. Aim for a decluttering milestone daily. Given some time, you will find that it's more about the plan than the work itself.

Why You Need a Cleaning Routine

Spend 10 minutes every day on a few daily tasks. That's an hour per week, and you even get to rest one day. Once you've developed a system, you may find yourself running on autopilot. This is good. This means you've freed up time to think. And it keeps your mind uncluttered. Save your energy for the fun stuff. This method isn't meant for busy lives – it's meant to take away the drudgery right out of cleaning. Challenge yourself to sticking with a cleaning routine. Cultivate good habits and build a good foundation. You'll find it more effortless, and it'll bring you the satisfaction which is most important.

DIY Projects vs. Store-Bought Products for Decluttering

Now, decluttering can go in different ways, you can approach your home improvement needs on your own, carrying out do-it-yourself projects; or you can go the straightforward path that involves obtaining all sorts of store-bought materials. Both will solve the issue you have with the clutter in your home. But the direction you take, will determine the precision at which you hit your personal goals.

In other words, your decision will depend on your priorities:

- Affordability. This depends on the materials and equipment you need to purchase, in order to fulfil a single project. If you have the tools and equipment lying around, that's good because you can use them for a lot of things. At the very least, you will require a bit of capital in the beginning of your journey; but as soon as you have everything you need, each project will cost less and less. Of course, there are some needs where store-bought items will prove more affordable than its DIY option. If cost is important to you, look at this closely.

- Availability. Of course, buying something is going to be easier than making one. If there is urgency with the need, and you think there is no room for delay that construction will definitely give—then buying will be the most practical solution. However, some designs make use of things that are most likely lying around in your house. It may involve some tweaking but you will be surprised to find how simple many of these projects are.

- Experience. Carrying out at a DIY project is definitely more enriching than taking your wallet out to shop. Every project your finish is going to bring fulfilment that's going to be beyond comparison. This is most especially true, once you see your finished product being used and someone applauds what you have done. Experience cannot be purchased in any way. The satisfaction you get after you complete something is something that you can hold to, for a very long time.

- Time and Effort. Of course, if you choose experience, it will demand that you devote time and effort to it. If you have a lot to spare, then that's good; but if you do not really have the luxury to sit down and labor on DIY projects, you are better off going to the store. It is definitely more demanding if you choose the DIY route—but you have to realize the value that's attached to it, the time and effort you put in, adds premium to anything you finish.

- Quality and Function. This is the trickiest factor to consider because many DIY projects can rival machine-made and store-bought items, depending on the skill of the maker. So, you have to look at yourself here. Do you think you can produce quality and functional items that can compare to store-bought items? Is the project technically demanding or is it fairly straightforward? If you think you can produce something of good quality and function, then go ahead.

- Personalization. While there are store-bought items that may be customized, they're often double the cost. If you are particular with aesthetics and dimensions, you can best achieve perfection with a self-made item. It is cheaper than to have something custom-made, and you will be more satisfied with the results.

Whichever route you take, is up to you. This book focuses on the do-it-yourself route because we believe in the enrichment it provides in terms of experience. When you are given the opportunity to exercise your creativity, you take advantage of this because your time and effort will give you affordable solutions that will more or less deliver the same function.

Every DIY project is labored from the heart and this dedication will make every item created, worth so much more when you give it a personal touch. This book organizes each project per room, so that you can plan your home improvement—one-room-at-a-time.

Chapter 2 - Starting Small

Simple Cleaning Must-Haves

Cleaning isn't complicated and the supplies you use shouldn't be, either. In fact, you will find yourself making most of the stuff here. And they get the job done. Less fanciful, less complications. This also leaves less of a dent on your wallet. And we have even more satisfaction – extra brownie points.

Below is a list of common cleaning must-haves:

- Dishwashing soap
- All-purpose cleaner
- Disinfecting cleaner
- Microfiber cleaning cloths
- Sponges
- Scrub Brushes
- Dusting wand
- Baking soda
- Mop
- Vacuum cleaner
- Toilet brush
- Bucket
- Caddy or tote

Daily, Weekly, Monthly, and Seasonal Cleaning Tasks

Sample Daily Tasks:

- Make beds
  As soon as you get up in the morning, pull up your beddings and fluff your pillows. This gets you off to a great start. One task down, and an instant gratification.

- Check floors
  You don't need to do the full throttle on this daily – sweep or vacuum as needed and as often as you can. This decreases your workload and prevents chores from piling up. And far less dirt to clean at any given time.

- Wipe counters
  These are some of the areas that get dirty and dusty. Wipe counters daily as time permits. Wipe tables after dinner. You can see where this going. Check bathroom counters before taking a shower. Tidy up your worktable after use.

- De-clutter
  Pick up clutter as soon as you see it. Don't let it sit and fester. A big mess can accumulate in the blink of an eye, if you don't address it in the first place.

- Do laundry
  If you can do it every couple of days, great. A week is still fine, but don't leave it longer than that. Or it will become daunting as it accumulates. And we want to remove any reason to keep us from doing what we have to do. Don't let the pile of clothes build up anywhere in the house. It looks bad, it smells bad, and it becomes another obstacle.

Sample Weekly Tasks:

- Monday - Bathrooms
  It is always great to start the week by tackling the most work. A clean bathroom is always a great start, as it tends to be the first place you visit to start the day. A fresh and clean bath area for the rest of the week will put you in good spirits.

- Tuesday – Dusting Day
  Dust weekly, and you will spend less time dusting. You don't even need to move everything around. Work from the top and move down bottom. Dust the hard surfaces, staircases, railings, tv, and furniture.

- Wednesday – Vacuuming Day
  Since you've done all the dusting on Tuesday, it makes sense to follow it with vacuuming the next day. Always start at the corner that's farthest from your front door and work your way there. You may vacuum as needed on other days of the week, but once a week at the very least prevents build up.

- Thursday – Floor Washing Day
  Now that you've done the dusting and vacuuming, it's time to focus on washing the floors and making them shine. Using a washable mop head or microfiber pad will help it avoid streaking and dulling.

- Friday – Miscellaneous
  Dedicate yourself one day in a week to perform all other tasks you weren't able to focus on from the other days. This is time to catch up if you have fallen behind. Make sure the week's tasks are up to date.

- Saturday – Sheets and Towels Day
  Since most of us have Saturdays off, this is the perfect day to do larger loads of laundry. This may include your bedsheets, pillowcases, curtains, and other linens.

- Sunday – Recharge Day
  Take a break – you deserve it!

Monthly and Seasonal Tasks

These are the tasks that don't need daily or weekly maintenance, but need addressing every now and then. These tasks may include:

- Cleaning light fixtures
- Washing rugs
- Cleaning oven, refrigerators, other appliances

- Washing windows
- Polishing wood furniture
- Replacing filters form the furnace, humidifier, air conditioner, etc.

Chapter 3 – How to Start Decluttering

Clutter doesn't take much to creep in and invade your home. Dealing with it daily is the only way to avoid the overwhelming feeling. Don't give piling up a chance. Every day you tackle puts you one step closer to being clutter-free.

Before you start de-cluttering, here are a few things you need to make it less of a chore and more of a fun activity for you:

- A set amount of time
  Whether you only have 10 minutes or 3 hours, you need work with gusto. Do what you can with the amount of time you have and you'll be further on than you were the day before.
- Bins and garbage bags
  For storing clutter and making it easy for you to dispose or sort them out later.
- Timer
  Setting up a timer can give you extra motivation and can challenge you to do more in the time that you have.
- Something to watch or listen to
  Put on some music. Listen to that podcast you've been wanting to get through. Watch that TV show your friends told you about. Now is the time to do it – killing two birds with one stone. And it makes decluttering fun.

Bathrooms

Sample products designed to help you declutter and organize your bathroom:

- Cosmetics organizers
- Customizable horizontal and vertical shelf dividers
- Layered hooks and Towel bars
- Shower caddies
- Vanity organizers

The bathroom is the sanctuary for taking care of your body. The place to give yourself a well-deserved relaxation from work and life stressors. This is your private space and it has to be clutter-free.

Check if you have enough waste baskets. Make sure these are well-covered with a retractable lid to keep the sight and odours away from plain view. Next, consider your shower caddy. Instead of keeping small ones, replace them with a large one. Get multi-tiers to keep your soaps and sponges organized.

Bath and hand towels all over the place? Put up racks for ones currently in use. Introduce a small basket or shelf where you can roll each towel in. You save space and can see everything in a glance.

Check the medicine cabinet for expired meds. Throw these ones out to make space for new and fresh medications. Organize and clean countertops by throwing out the ones that are not used at most of the time. Place dividers inside the drawers to separate belongings in the same category. Use decorative holders or bath baskets to tackle hair dryers and curling irons.

Living Spaces

Sample products designed to help you declutter and organize your living room:
- Stacking end tables
- Nesting TV trays
- Gaming stands
- Magazine racks
- Bookcases

Different people have different living rooms. Keep in mind your own unique needs and wants when going through the process of decluttering. Adding furniture may seem counter-productive, but they can help organise the room. Take a careful look around and check if you need to put in a magazine stand, or a coat rack. A nice-looking chest can also double as a coffee table to save space and store some items.

If you are fond of providing entertainment, or if you have kids in the house, a nesting table can come handy. Have one table or desk for playing cards, jigsaw puzzles, or making crafts in one corner of the living room. Place a box on the focal point in the living room. The assortment of items that tend to be around can all be placed in this one spot.

If reading is your thing, set up bookshelves or magazine racks so books don't get strewn all over the place. Use vertical shelves to store music and movies collection. Get a big chest for toys so the kids can clean up after playing.

Check out the hall closet next to your living room. Is there clutter everywhere? Keep the hallways free of any obstruction. This improves functionality as well as the aesthetic appeal.

Bedrooms

Sample products designed to help you declutter and organize your bedroom:
- Shoe racks
- Jewellery organizers
- Clothing bins
- Shoe racks
- Jewellery organizers
- Drawers with organizers and dividers
- DIY customizable closets
- Specialty hangers and hooks

Sort through your clothes and weed out the ones that are no longer of use. Put away clothes that are seasonal or aren't worn. Follow a rule wherein you choose to throw or give out anything that you haven't worn in a year or two. This way, you simplify your decision making. Only you can decide which time frame to use, and be sure to stick to it.

Categorize your hanging clothes into groups. One side for the long ones, and the other for the short ones. Underneath the short hanging clothes, you can place a basket, a shoe rack, or other handy storage units. Subdivide your clothes according to type. This will bring about a clean and organized aesthetic in your closet.

Buy adjustable horizontal closet rods that you can use to hang small things. Add a hanging bag made of lightweight plastic for socks. Make sure it's narrow enough to fit into the spaces between your rods. Use same principle for storing shoes. Use a hanging shoe rack where you can store shoes away from plain sight. This should be accessible so that you can retrieve them from your closet.

If a jumble of socks, underwear, or scarves is a common sight in your drawer, then it's time to take action. Make use of customizable drawer dividers and line these up inside your drawer. Sort your items according to kind and keep them separate from the other categories.

Make use of pegboards or magnifying strips to keep jewellery organized.

Kitchen

Sample products designed to help you declutter and organize your kitchen:

- Silverware trays
- Expandable shelves
- Pots and pans hangers
- Drawer dividers
- Netting plasticware
- Vertical shelf dividers
- Stemware hangers
- Food storage bins
- Recipe filers
- Coupon organizers
- Tiered spice racks

Install collapsible shelving, rotating circular shelves and hooks. This can help you use dead space. Pay attention to installed drawer and cabinet organizers in your kitchen. These can hold rows and rows of stuff that you may be of great use to you when you take time to organize your kitchen.

Throw or donate any unused pots or pans lids. The goal is to keep only quality cookware that is actually of use to you. It is best to put the largest items on the bottom and add in the smaller pots and pans when working your way up. Keep lids separate on a rack inside the kitchen door cabinet with an installed shelf. Use wire shacks to add space and provide height to the kitchen. If you have large wall that is spacious enough, install pegs and hang your pots and pans on this wall. There is no need to buy another shelf, and this will help you save money and space. A lazy Susan can benefit corner. Pots and pans can be locatable on its rotating shelf.

Installing a magnetic knife bar in place that's easily visible. This will stop you from getting hurt from sharp edges. You may also keep any utensils on this bar even if it's plastic, as long as you apply a little stick-on of magnet on its surface.

Plastic bottles are usually present in kitchens. Do your part in reducing plastic waste by recycling these items and making them useful. Cut off their tops, and create a new container for storing raw pasta or pet food.

Instead of stacking dishes in a horizontal fashion, try to find a way to get those vertical stacks. Regain all that precious countertop space. There are several stack-them-up yourself shelves, where you can save yourself some money.

Create subdivisions inside your pantry space where you can sort items by type. For example, you can keep all dry grains together in one place, and all the canned goods in another. Knowing what goes where can be much easier for you to find things. Make it a point to find a place for everything that deserves to be there. Once you have set up a place for these things to go, you won't have to do this part again.

Garage

Sample products designed to help you declutter and organize your garage:

- Tool racks
- Tool boxes Plastic file boxes
- Pocketed gear holders
- Multi-use storage racks
- Layered storage pallets
- Storage boxes and bins
- Wall-control pegboards
- Customizable shelving
- Heavy wall clips and other utility storage items
- Large storage bins
- Wall boards
- Pocketed gear holders
- Customizable shelving
- Bicycle hangers

Organize tools according to their category. Place them in storage bins with labels or clear plastic containers. They should be identifiable should you need them.

Miscellaneous

Sample products to organize your laundry and office supplies:

- Hampers
- Collapsible shelving
- Various totes
- Laundry sorters
- Racks
- Collapsible towel racks
- Filing cabinets
- Paper management filers
- Sticky pads
- Utensil trays
- Stand-along vertical dividers
- Drawer organizers
- Magnet boards
- Bulletin boards
- Media and electronic storage products

A cluttered desk is a sign of a cluttered mind. To increase your productivity, clean up your work area. Find a container for your pens, notes, clips, and other small office supplies. Have trays available for your scratch pads and business cards.

Consider getting a smaller sized desk lamp if it takes too much space on your table. Check your wall space and find ways to make negative space more functional. Install products such as mail organizers, file pockets, memo boards, or key racks.

Are cords and cables cluttering your work space? Bring out those cable clamps and twist wires to segregate and put them in order.

What to Do with Your Clutter

There are four cardinal rules to follow when you declutter. Make it habit to put everything you come across into one of these categories.:

Keep
These are the items that you are keeping in the same area where you found them. Or if you do manage to find a more organized shelf for these items, even better. The trick is not about minimizing stuff, but knowing how to store or display them.

Donate/Sell
Making money out of things that you're not using is a great option. You may also choose to donate them to charities and other organizations.

Toss
This is the bag to throw stuff away. Put them in a recycling bin if it is applicable.

Move
This box is for anything that is in the wrong spot. You may also opt to rent out a storage facility area to hold these items.

Chapter 4 – DIY Projects for the Home

Your home is your personal sanctuary. It doesn't matter how you live outside, but when you come into your house, it is your personal space which is supposed to bring you comfort. Clutter is the kind of mess that has the potential to bring stress. Apart from it being messy and unsightly, it causes unnecessary disruption in your brain. It is important, therefore, for you to keep your home clutter free.

And to make this whole experience so much more worthwhile, this book is going to teach you valuable DIY projects that you can use to organize the clutter lying around in your home. A clean home is a healthy home. It promotes a state of physical, mental, emotional, and social well-being that is definitely desirable.

If you are not particularly an arts-and-crafty kind of person, it's okay. Most of these DIY projects are designed to be easy and perfect for newbie crafters. You do not have to be an experienced carpenter who's handy with power tools. As a matter of fact, you can even invite younger individuals to join in with the crafting, so that they can have something productive to do. This also provides valuable constructive family time together.

It's going to be fun and easy, so do not fret. But in case you're worried, here are some quick tips that you can use for your DIY journey:

1. Follow the instructions carefully. All throughout this book, you will be given simple instructions to follow, so that you may

complete every project with ease. You don't have to be a skilled worker, as many of these projects are fairly straightforward and will require little to no technical know-how. Regardless of your level of expertise, you just need to follow the instructions. And hopefully, by being very precise you will accomplish everything.

2. Use the right tools as often as you can, in order to arrive at the best possible finished product. Being resourceful is good because you are able to exercise your creativity and stretch your ability, in accordance to what is needed. But sometimes the margin of error becomes wider when you use to wrong tools and equipment.

3. Do not be afraid to give to give it your personal touch. If you think something needs to be changed with the design, to best fit your aesthetic and functional requirement, go ahead. What's important is that you are happy and proud at what you've accomplished.

4. If you make a mistake, just do it again. Even experienced crafters and carpenters make mistakes, from time to time, so be a little forgiving towards yourself if you commit an error. You have to keep going because this is a good thing you're doing—succeeding at decluttering will be a mountainous achievement.

5. Always value your safety above everything. At all times, never put yourself in danger. Do not attempt to do anything that can potentially bring you harm. If you're going to use tools and

equipment that you're relatively unfamiliar with, you are better off asking help from someone who knows how to operate it, rather than to use it yourself and incur an accident with it.

6. Endeavor to finish what you have started. Regardless of whether do-it-yourself projects are your cup of tea or not, you need to be the kind of person who decides to finish what's been started. You cannot pick something up, only to throw it away, when you do not want anything to do with it anymore. You have to be the type of person who is committed, and with decluttering, so much dedication and commitment to follow through is required in order to succeed in it. You cannot organize something today and not carry-on with the new arrangements. You have to follow through. If you want your home to be free from clutter, it is going to be a daily decision to keep the mess away.

But mostly, you need to have fun, because organizing does not have to be boring. It does not have to be laborious and demanding. It can be bucketloads of fun, especially if you do it with other people. This book is going to be your decluttering bible. It is going to lead your expedition from messy to organized, and it is going to change your life, forever.

"Success is no accident. It is hard work, perseverance, learning, studying, sacrifice and most of all, love of what you are doing or learning to do."

- Pele

Chapter 5 - DIY Projects for Decluttering your Bathroom

The toilet and bathroom, like the kitchen, is a highly functional room. Whether or not this space you are trying to work with is for personal use, it is important that you find a way to keep things clean and orderly. The toilet and bathroom tend to be quite messy, especially if a lot of people are using it. There will be personal hygiene products of all shapes and sizes that will be quite overwhelming if you do not have a proper place for them.

There are many potential problems that you can encounter with the toilet and bathroom—presence of unsightly clutter, abundance of trash, and a discomforting foul odor. Your inability to address these issues will define the level of dissatisfaction you and your visitors will feel when they use this room. It is important, therefore, that you pay attention to these helpful strategies to solve your clutter problems in the toilet and bathroom.

Magnetic Strips

Supplies:
Magnetic strips

Instructions:
Cut the strips to size and press them on the side of your medicine cabinet. Stick on small items such as bobby pins, tweezers, or nail files.

Hair Appliances Holder

Supplies:
3x3x2 45degree wye PVC Pipe
Spray paint of your colour of choice
Newspaper
Permanent paint markers

Instructions:
Lay out newspaper and spray the pipe according to your preference. You may also personalize it further by adding decors or glitter or drawings.
Let dry completely.
Use the pvc openings to hold your hair dryer or curling wands and their cords by allowing this pvc pipe to stand on its own. Or you can use a straight pipe, attach some adhesive on one side and glue it inside your cabinet door. You can then store your hair appliances the same way, only hanging.

Basket for Storage

Supplies:
Drill
Screw driver
Level
Measuring tape
Pencil
Putty knife, paint roller, paint tray (if needed)
Towel bars
Baskets
Spackling
Sand paper
Craft ribbon to attach baskets to bar or S-hooks

Instructions:

Attach towel bars according to instructions. Drill some holes, screwing in mounting hardware, then attach the bar to the hardware.

After the bars are up, cut up some ribbons and loop these through the baskets. Then tie the ribbons around the bar. Do the same for the rest of the baskets.

Place toiletries in one basket case, hand towels in another, and wash cloths in yet another.

The Old Suitcase Vanity (Medicine Cabinet)

Do you have a rusty old suitcase/luggage that you want to get rid of? It doesn't have to look so good as a travel companion, anymore, but surely can be good for something else. The space it provides is good enough and its sturdy design makes it truly reliable, so why waste it?

Every toilet and bathroom should be equipped with a medicine cabinet or vanity because it will house your medicines, grooming paraphernalia, and other toiletries. It is often placed above the sink, at eye level, so that it is easily accessed by anyone.

This organization design is going to give your bathroom a very quirky look that's perfect if you love to travel.

Supplies:

Old suitcase/luggage

Double-sided tape

Old map/wrapping paper

Small glass/plastic

Pieces of wood

Paint (white or any color)

Drill and screws

Instructions:

Line the inside of the suitcase. You can do two layers, using two different designs, so there is a nice contrast of colors. A first layer is made to fill the entirety of the case, up to the edges. The second layer will only line the innermost part of the suitcase. In the photo, a checkered wrapping paper was used for the first layer and a map was used for the second layer. Feel free to change the designs, according to your preferred theme or aesthetic.

Create shelving partitions using small pieces of wood. Paint the wood in white, or any color you desire. Measure the space and cut the wood evenly. Then position them horizontally, at your desired height, and glue them in place. Make sure that you can still shut the suitcase tight, even with the newly installed partitions.

Bolt the shelves to the wall. Choose the perfect place for your suitcase vanity and drill them onto the wall. Make sure that you put enough screws so that the suitcase can carry the weight of its contents.

Leave the outside part of the suitcase as it is, even if you think it looks worn and tattered. The "worn out" look is going to give it a very cool appearance, especially when it's bolted on the wall. People are going to be wondering, *"What is this suitcase doing hanging on the wall?"* And when they open it, they will surely be amazed.

Towel and Plate Rack

It's always a good idea when you are able to convert something purely decorative, into something functional too. In this design option, you are turning a relatively useless but pretty plate rack, into a functional towel rack. It doesn't just have to be a rack holding decorative plates—you can also prettily hang your towels on these racks.

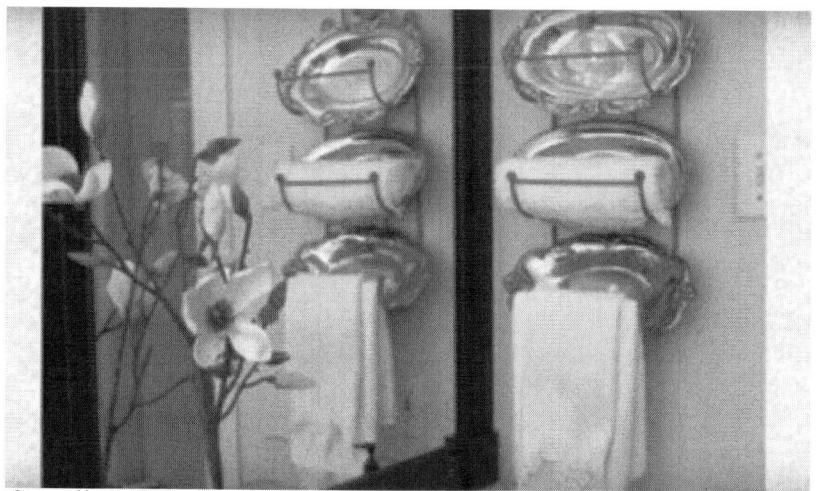

Supplies:
Decorative plate rack
Decorative plates
Hand towels
Drill and screws

Instructions:
Find plates that you use wish to use as décor and find a wall-mounted rack that will house the plates that you have chosen to hang.
Bolt the racks onto the wall, preferably by the sink used for washing hands

Lay the plates on the rack, you normally would.
On the bottom rack, hang a towel loosely, so that it may be used conveniently for hand drying. On the racks above it, lay rolled-up and unused hand towels on them, so you can easily replace soiled towels with a fresh one.

Turning a mere plate rack into a towel rack escalates its value. From a purely senseless item, it is now quite useful in the bathroom.

Personalized Oral Hygiene Tray

Oral hygiene is important if you want to maintain the health and beauty of your smile.

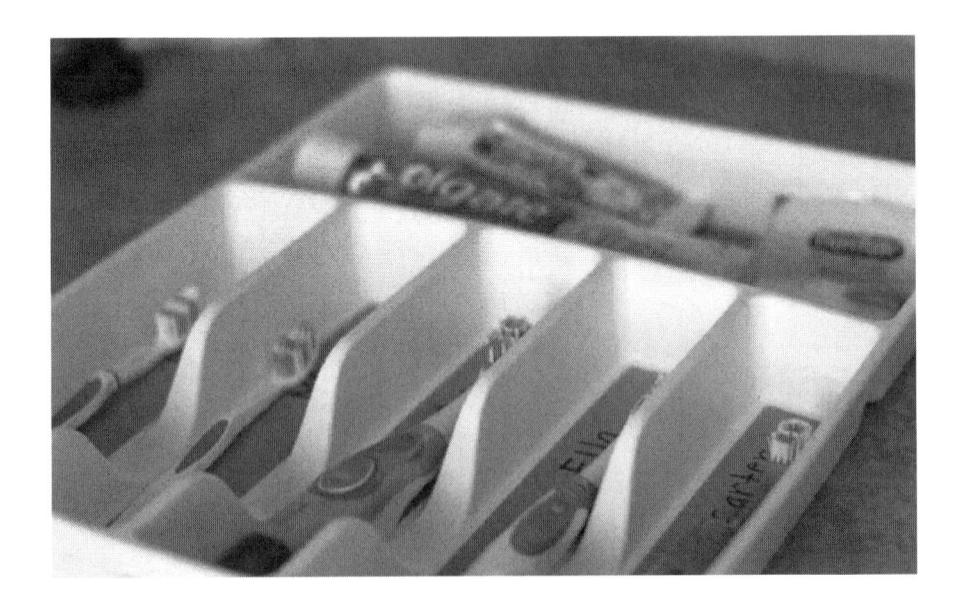

Supplies:
Organizing tray
Labeler

Oral hygiene essentials

Instructions:
Find an organizing tray with enough slots to fit all the toothbrush you need to hold
Label each slot with the person's name and this is where you put the toothbrushes. But leave 1-2 slots empty for the toothpaste and floss sticks.

This is not a common way to store oral hygiene paraphernalia but this is a creative and inexpensive way to keep things organized.

Under the Sink

The area under the sink, where the pipes are, is a highly under-utilized area. It is often messy and wet, especially if plumbing is not as superb as you would hope for it to be. Finding a way to use a traditionally useless space is going to change your decluttering game, altogether.

Supplies:
Metal racks/containers
Metal or plastic baskets

Instructions:
Clean the area under the sink. If this is not as clean as it is supposed to be, you need to make it spic-and-span before you use it as storage space.
Buy two metal shower racks and line them, facing each other, on either side of the cabinet.
Buy a plastic or metal basket and put it in the middle of the two racks. Organize all your toiletries, grooming tools, and medicines into the different racks and basket.

This area under the sink, behind the cabinet doors, is often a forgotten area and you're learning to transform it to something useful. This will keep things clean and organized; and if you're creative enough, you can store a lot of things in this space.

Hanging Bathroom Toys

Do you have bathroom toys lying around and making a big mess in the toilet and bath? Do you often trip and slip on any of these bathroom toys and although you want to dump them in the bin, you know your precious child needs it for bath time? Well, you just have to think a good way to pack them away when they're not being used.

Supplies:
Mesh bag
Suction hook

Instructions:

To avoid drilling holes and to conveniently replace the hooks in various areas around the toilet and bathroom, you may use a suction hook that you need to just wet and stick on to a clean tile.

Get your mesh bag and contain all the bathroom toys in it. Close to secure it and hang it on the hook.

You do not have to be stressed about rubber duckies littered on the tub, the sink, the floor anymore. All the toys will be in the mesh bag.

Filing Your Tissues and Stuff

Here's another creative use for your desk organizers. Why spend so much for those fancy tissue holders when you can buy one from your favourite office supplies store, right?

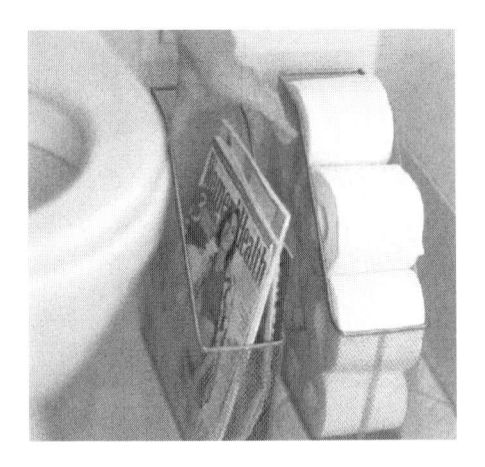

Supplies:
Desk organizer
Tissue papers rolls
Magazines

Instructions:

Get yourself a few desk organizers

Use it to contain your stock of tissue paper, magazines, or even your towels.

You can use this idea to keep your things conveniently "filed" in the toilet and bathroom.

Over-the-Sink Organizer

Here's a good idea for containers, for all the bathroom knick knacks that you have—toothbrush, cotton buds, makeup brushes, hairbrush, lotions, and so forth. Some people have medicine cabinets under the mirror, and maybe you're not the type that goes for that. Maybe your sink is small and you do not really have enough space for most of your things, so this is why this is going to work.

Supplies:
Wood
Wood saw
Sandpaper

Wood glue
Varnish and brush

Instructions:
Determine how many containers you need because this will dictate your design, and therefore, the materials that you require
Prepare the wood that you will need. You will need three long rectangular sheets that will form the front, bottom, and back of the case. You will also need two square wooden pieces of the sides and several smaller square sheets that will function as dividers.
Assemble the case with wood glue. Make sure it is secure enough to hold what you're going to put in it.
Sand it until it is smooth and apply wood varnish on the surface to give it a brilliant polish.
Bolt the case to the wall, making sure it is secure.
Arrange your toiletries and grooming tools into each compartment.

This project is best installed under the mirror and above the sink, so that you can easily get to your things. Varnish is used in this example but feel free to use paint, if you would rather give it more character.

Bottle Me Up

Commercial bottles of shampoo, conditioner, lotion, and soap aren't pleasing to the eye because they come in random shapes and sizes. This idea is a great aesthetic improvement to beautify your washing area.

Supplies:
Bottles
Labeler

Instructions:
Gather all the liquid products in your bathroom—shampoo, conditioner, body wash, hand wash, lotion and so forth.
Obtain reusable bottles where you can transfer the contents of the commercial into.
Create labels for each bottle, so that you can identify them easily.

Maintaining similar bottles for every liquid product you have in the toilet and bathroom makes things look organized and tidy.

Hanging Basket

This basket is often found in the kitchen but can also be used in the bathroom to provide more organization. Instead of letting the clutter mess up the toilet and bath, you can pile them onto one of these hanging baskets. You may buy this ready-made, but it is quite easy to make one in case you can't get your hands on it.

Supplies:
Metal basket
Metal string

Instructions:

Find metal baskets. About 3-4 pieces will do, depending on how big they are and how much space you have in the toilet and bath
Get a metal string and if it's not strong or thick enough, you can reinforce it by coiling it together. Otherwise you may start building your multi-level basket. Draw one metal string on one side, and attach one basket on top of the other, with enough space in between. Get another string and do the same on another side, from the bottom basket to the top one. Get one more string and connect the baskets on one side. When you get to the topmost basket, gather a considerable length of the metal string and bring them together. Twist the three strings to form one, and then create a knot or hook.
Attach the basket to one end of the shower curtain rod. Arrange the bath accessories and toys in the baskets.

If you would rather use plastic, you may. Plastic is easier to clean and it does not rust, so it may be best used in a damp toilet and bath.

Color-Coded Towels

If your bathroom is being used by more than one person, towels often get mixed up, especially when they are of the same color. This idea is simple but effective because the color codes are attached to the towel.

Supplies:
Towels
Different color strings
Hooks
Needle and thread

Instructions:
Determine how many towels you need to have in the bathroom
Prepare one color of cloth for every towel that you have and sew it on the towel, rolling the cloth slightly, to create some kinds of knot
Obtain hooks if your washroom doesn't already have some. You may use plastic hooks, or you may bolt wooden hooks to the wall.
Hang each towel to the hook

This allows you to have uniformly colored towels while being able to be distinguish them from each other in an efficient manner.

Cotton Bottles

Instead of keeping many different cotton products in their original packaging, why not put them together in a small container? This works for cotton buds, cotton balls, and cotton pads. You may even include band-aid and gauze. Keeping the in container will keep them dry and enable easy access.

Supplies:
Containers
Cotton products
Labeler

Instructions:
Determine what products you wish to contain. Cotton balls, cotton buds, cotton pads, band-aids, gauze, and so forth
Provide one container for each product. The container may be made of plastic or glass. Make sure it is easy to open and close
For easy identification, put labels on each container.

You may keep the containers inside the medicine cabinet or on top of the counter.

Towel Files

Here's another good use for file organizers. If you do not know where to put your face towels, you can stack on inside a file organizer and put the organizer in one corner of the toilet and bath—where it can stay dry and clean when not in use.

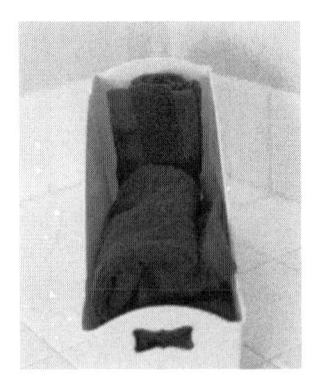

Supplies:
File organizer
Face towels

Instructions:
Find a plastic file organizer that's no longer in use
Roll the towels like burrito
Stack the towel burritos on top of each other, inside the file organizer

Now it's easy for you to get a towel when you need it.

Hair Equipment Organizer

We all know how important our hair is to use, and many of you probably have loads of equipment and styling products that you use. Perhaps you have blow dryers, curling irons and flat irons. Not storing them properly can lead to lots of clutter, especially with loads of cords and wires.

Supplies:
Shower rack
Drill and screws

Instructions:
Find a shower rack. This is usually hung or bolted by the shower, so you can put the large bottles of shampoo, conditioner and body wash. Bolt this on the backside of the door of your sink cabinet. Make sure it is secure enough to carry its load.
Arrange the hair equipment on the bolted rack. Coil the cord around and stuff each one of them into one of the slots that are meant for bottles.

Simple ideas are often the best. This allows you to keep things organized underneath your bathroom sink.

Cabinet Under the Sink

Standalone sinks are pretty, but building a cabinet under the sink is going to be really useful. It's not bolted or attached to the sink, so you can always revert back to how things were if you decide it is not your cup of tea.

Supplies:
Wood
Wood saw
Paint and brush
Sandpaper
Hinge and screw
Hammer and nails
Cabinet door/knob

Instructions:
Design the cabinet around the sink. Prepare the wood pieces that you are going to use. You will need one large rectangular piece for the back of the cabinet, two rectangular sheets of wood to form the sides, two narrower sheets of rectangular pieces that will form the doors of the cabinets. You will need two shorter rectangular pieces to form the top and bottom of the cabinet.
Assemble the cabinet—putting together the different pieces of wood that you have prepared. Make sure that every piece is secured with

nails. You want a sturdy cabinet that's going to hold your important bathing things.

Attach the door of the cabinet with a hinge and make sure that it opens and closes with much ease.

Run sandpaper on the surface of the wood, to make it smooth; and apply paint to fix the appearance of the cabinet.

Create the notch that will allow you to fit the sink into the shape of the cabinet.

Attach the cabinet handles/knobs to the doors. Make sure it is secure.

Arrange the contents inside the cabinet.

Toilet Paper Holder

Toilet paper holders are common things; and they're usually placed in front of the toilet, as they are most accessible that way. Unfortunately, not a lot of people like how a toilet paper holder is exposed.

Supplies:
Toilet paper holder

Instructions:
Bolt the tissue holder on the side of the toilet bowl
Attach the toilet paper on the holder

This idea is very simple, really. By making the decision to have the toilet paper holder tucked away in the corner, it will not clutter the toilet anymore.

Sideways Baskets on the Wall

Here's a simple idea that will give you a place for small towels. It's basically floating shelves, without actually constructing shelves. In lieu of wood, you can use ready-made baskets and simply bolt them to the wall.

Supplies:
Metal baskets
Drill and screws
Towels

Instructions:
Find an empty wall, in the toilet in bath, where you can arrange the baskets. Determine how many baskets you will need to contain your towels.
Bolt the baskets from the bottom, so that it is hanging sideways from the wall
Fold or roll the towels and arrange them properly into the baskets

You can also decorate the basket to make them more appealing. Attach artificial plants and flowers through the slots so that the baskets will be more than just metal cages.

Corner Shelf

The corner is under-utilized but it's fairly valuable space that you can use. If you are going to consider getting proper shelving for your toiletries, you should consider getting one that's designed for the corner, so that you can use the space effectively.

Supplies:
Corner shelf
Drill and screws

Instructions:
Bolt the corner shelf to the area nearest the showers, so you can easily reach to your favourite shampoo and conditioner, while taking a shower. Make sure the shelf is secure on the wall and that it is strong enough to carry the heavy bottles.
Arrange the bottles neatly on the shelves, making sure they're properly spaced

There are different types of shelves and containers that you can use for the bathroom, but this design allows you the illusion of more space.

Hanging Mesh Case

Instead of using a traditional bolted shelf, you can use a simple mesh container that basically hangs like a shower curtain. Like a curtain, it has slots through which you attach shower curtain rings, so that you may hang them alongside the actual shower curtain.

Supplies:
Mesh fabric
Piping material (plastic)
Plastic fabric
Scissors
Needle and thread

Instructions:
Prepare the mesh cloth for this particular design. You'll need a large one to form the framework of the entire design. You also need smaller square pieces of the same mesh cloth, to be able to form the pouches that should hold your different toiletries.
Prepare the piping that should hold the mesh cloth securely, at the edges.
Prepare the plastic fabric and cut holes into it. This should form the top part of the mesh case that's going to hang to the rod with the rings.
Assemble the pieces you've prepared and make sure that everything is tightly secure so that it can hold its contents.
Arrange everything into the pouches and hang it on the shower curtain rod.

You use mesh because it doesn't get too wet. This kind of material dries easily and is easy to clean, making it perfect for use in the toilet and bath.

Hanging Glass Shelf

Floating shelves are great because they provide extra storage without taking up much space. These work great in the toilet and bathroom, between the mirror and the sink.

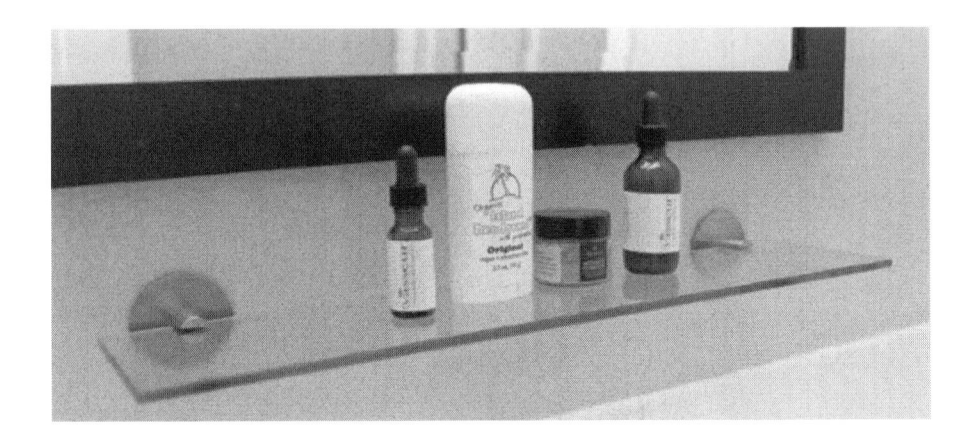

Supplies:
Wall bracket
Glass shelf
Drill and screw

Instructions:
Determine the size of glass shelf you will need for the toilet and bath. It should be shorter than the width of the mirror, but long enough to contain a number of things.
Bolt the brackets to the wall. They should be positioned wide apart enough to provide proper support to the length of the shelf, but near enough so that it fits. You should also make sure that the two brackets are levelled so that the shelf stands even and parallel to the floor.
Attach the glass shelf to the bracket. Making sure it is secure enough so that the glass doesn't slip off.

Arrange your things on the shelf, but be careful not to put on too much weight on it.

Floating shelves sophisticated, aesthetically pleasing and easily accessible. They are the crux of a modern home and makes the most of space available.

Towel in Wine Holders

Maybe you have an old wine holder that you're about to get rid of. Instead of chucking it in the trash, you could give it a renewed purpose.

Supplies:
Wine holder

Towels

Instructions:
Clean the old wine holder/stand
Get your towels, roll them like a burrito, and lay one towel each into one of the slots.

You can put the wine holder/rack on the bathroom counter. This makes it highly accessible and you can grab a fresh towel whenever you need one.

Ladder Shelving

Do you wish to install some kind of shelf at the back of your toilet? It is, after all, wasted space that you can utilize efficiently. And if you are looking for ideas on how to do just that, then this simple ladder design fits the bill.

Supplies:
Wood
Wood saw
Sandpaper
Hammer and nails

Instructions:

Decide on the design of the ladder so you can prepare the wood. You will basically need two large rectangular blocks that will form the legs of the ladder; and you will need two shorter rectangular pieces that will form the rungs of the ladder.

Assemble the ladder, making sure that there is a wide space between the legs. Make sure the rungs of the ladder are secure, before you put anything on them

Arrange your things on the ladder. You can use it for your towels; but you can also hang some baskets and plants, to give it colour.

Plastic Containers

A fully-stocked medicine cabinet could cause quite the mess. The best way to organise all of them would be to divide them into plastic containers. You can label them for ease of identification at a glance.

Supplies:
Plastic containers
Labeler

Instructions:

Gather all your medication and sort them accordingly. As soon as you've organized what you have, you will know how many separate containers you will need.

Contain the medicines and whatnot, into their appropriate containers. Provide a label for each case.

Mirror and Toilet Storage

Common medicine cabinets have mirrors in the front, so that they could serve two purposes. But sometimes you may decide that the mirror is too small or the cabinet is too cramped, so this design solves both issues. You can have a full-length mirror installed that opens to a shelved cabinet.

Supplies:
Full-length mirror
Wood
Wood saw
Sandpaper
Wood varnish and brush
Hinge and screws
Drill
Cabinet handle

Instructions:
Find good enough space in the toilet and bath, where you can build a cabinet.
Saw into the wall. This wall should be of considerable depth, and it is best when you can have it near the sink.
Prepare the various pieces of wood that you will need to build the cabinet. You will need four large rectangular pieces to form the walls of the cabinet, a few short pieces to form the shelves, two large sheets of wood to form the sides of the frames of the mirror, and two short rectangular sheets to form the upper and lower part of the mirror frame.
Assemble the cabinet and make sure it is secure enough to carry its potential contents.
Assemble the mirror and cover of the cabinet. Attach the mirror to the door of the last piece of wood—making sure it is properly bolted and encage it with the sheets of wood, to sort of frame the entire thing.
Attach the door to the whole structure with a hinge.
Run sandpaper through the surface and apply varnish.
Attach the handle

Now you can have a full-length storage that can contain not just medicines and toiletries but towels and various linens as well.

Cabinet Frames

Supplies:
Picture frame
Wooden sheets
Wood saw
Sandpaper
Hinge and screw

Instructions:
Find yourself a nice picture frame of a considerable size
Decide where you want to build your hidden storage. Saw the wall in, to create space to build shelves
Attach the picture frame to cover the hidden shelf you've created, with a hinge

Secret Bath Tub Storage

To maximize space, we just have to be a little creative. Installing secret bath tub storage on the sides will do the trick.

Supplies:
Wood
Wood saw
Hinge and bracket
Hinge lock
Metal trays
Drawer handles
Drill and screws
Hammer and nails

Instructions:

Measure the size of the bathtub, as it will dictate the size of wood you are going to prepare to build your hidden storage

Prepare the wood. You will need one large rectangular sheet to cover the length of the bathtub, and a shorter one to cover the width. You also need a few rectangular blocks to build the frame of the hidden cabinets: a long one to frame the length of the longer side, a shorter one to frame the length of the shorter side, and three more to frame the height of the three corners.

Attach the trays on the back surface of the walls. Provide enough to hold your shampoo, conditioner and body wash.

Assemble the cabinet walls/casing and the frames, making sure it is secure

Attach the hinge mechanism and the locks. Make sure that it opens wide enough so that you can easily get anything you need while taking a bath.

Attach the handles

The positioning of the hidden drawers is good because you can easily get hold of whatever you need, without needing to stand up.

Pull-Out Side Cabinets

Here's another hidden cabinet idea that's going to get rid of your clutter, in the most creative way. Instead of the common medicine cabinet, you can use this to effectively organize your things at the back of the mirror.

Supplies:
Mirror
Wood
Wood saw

Sandpaper
Paint and brush
Gliding mechanism
Metal drawer handles
Hammer and nails
Drill and screws

Instructions:

Prepare the wood that you're going to use. You will need two large rectangular pieces of wood to form the base of the cabinet and the base of the mirror/door of the cabinet. You will also need pieces of wood to build the drawer, shelves and frame of the mirror.

Assemble the shelf/drawer part of the design. You need two rectangular sheets to form the base of the drawers on either side, smaller sheets of wood to form the shelves, and a thicker rectangular piece of wood to form the door of the drawer or the sides of the cabinet. Finally, you need smaller sheets of wood to form the shelves. Attach the smaller metal handles to each shelf to serve as barrier; and attach the two larger handles to the sides of the cabinet.

Build the mirror by attaching the mirror to the large piece of wood, and assemble the frame around the mirror on its four sides.

Assemble the casing by bringing together the base, the top, bottom and cover/mirror.

Run sandpaper to smoothen the surface and apply paint to the woof Attach the gliding mechanism to the drawers. Make sure it opens and closes with ease.

Arrange your things inside the cabinet. You may use small containers to fully organize its contents.

Chapter 6 - DIY Projects for Decluttering your Living Space

The living room is the first room that is seen when anyone enters the house. As soon as the front door opens, the person is welcomed into the living room. Some people will have a quaint patio just before the door opens or they will have a foyer with a corridor that leads to the actual living room; but ultimately it is the first room that anyone sees. So, for this reason, the living room should provide a warm welcome not just to your visitors, but to you as well.

Clutter is not going to give a relaxing picture for anyone coming in, so you should deal with the mess it makes. You have to fix your living room so that it gives a kind of warmth that embraces and soothes. After a busy day at work, you want to come into the house to relax. Mess is not going to be good for your sanity, so you need to carryout effective organizing strategies that will hide, arrange or completely eradicate the clutter in your room.

If you're ready, here are some decluttering designs you can try.

Hanging Garden

Supplies:
4-5-inch terracotta flower pots
¾ inch pine boards
Rope
Zip ties
RYOBI 18-volt cordless drill
Milwaukee 4-inch Bi-metal Hole saw
RYOBI 18-volt circular saw
Husky 7-inch Diagonal pliers

Instructions:

Lay out the holes. Using a pencil, mark out the locations of the holes on a board. Leave about 2" between each flower pot hole, as well as about 1" between the rope holes and edges of the board.

Cut the boards. Establish the holes in their locations. Trim the boards to your desired length.

Put plot holes. Drill some plot holes through an entire stack of boards. Ensure everything is aligned.

Make holes for pots. Using both hands and setting your drill to the highest mode, make out holes that will fit each pot.

Drill holes for rope, ensuring them to have a tight fit that will keep the zip ties tied together.

Sand the boards using an orbital sander and a 220-grit paper.

String the boards together by stringing ropes through each hole. Make a secure knot at the bottom.

Hang and secure the boards. Make sure you are putting enough space for the plants between boards. You can use zip ties to keep boards in place.

Display your plants and enjoy admiring them! A vertical hanging shelf like this can save space.

Behind the Pictures

Keys are necessary and they are best stored by the main door in your living room. Unfortunately, the clutter of keys can be so unsightly, so why not try this behind-the-pictures-trick with your keys. You can store all kinds of keys behind the frame—car keys, office keys, and all the different keys to the rooms in the house.

Supplies:

Frame

Hooks

Labeler

Hinge and bracket

Instructions:

Find a frame that's big enough to hide all the keys you want to organize. It can be a painting or work of art; or it can be a photograph. Measure the frame against the wall to determine how much space you have.

Screw in the hooks onto the wall. Make sure they are spaced properly, so that you can hang the keys properly.

Label each hook accordingly. This will give every set of keys an assigned hook, so that you can tell right away, if anything is out of place. More so, this kind of organization makes it easier for you to get to the right set of keys, even when you're in a hurry.

Install the hinge and bracket at the precise area so that you can creatively hide the keys using your frame of choice. Screw in the frame with the hinge and bracket.

Hang the keys onto their assigned hooks.

Keys have the be organized because they need to be highly accessible to you. Keeping them in one place, in an organized manner, increase ease and functionality; the trick to hide them behind the frame is a nifty disappearing act. Just remember you put them there!

DIY Charging Station

Supplies:
Cardboard storage box
Book plates with eyelets
Small brads
Power board
Craft knife
Sharp pointed items for punching holes
Pencil
Paint
Ruler

Instructions:

On your box, mark and measure where you want to place the book plates.

Cut out the rectangles and give a quick file to tidy up some of the raggedy edges. Using a big needle, punch the holes needed for the brads.

Place the chargers inside the box and place the cords so they stick out of the designated holes.

The design of the box is to conceal cords in a manageable container. Make sure to turn off the power board off the wall when it's not in use.

Guest Charging Station

With the very digital life we all live in, charging phones and other gadgets have become a basic necessity. When a person enters a room or establishment, he immediately locates the most accessible electrical outlet. Why not give them an actual place to charge?

Supplies:
An unused outlet in the living room
Small curtain rod
Hooks
Metal flower pots
Metal basket
Metal tray

Instructions:
Bolt a small curtain rod just below an unused electrical outlet
Install 4 metal hooks and hang flower pots on these hooks to elevate the aesthetic appeal of this design
Hang a metal basket in the middle of 2 flower pots
On a metal tray, write the words, "Charge Here" and place this tray at the bottom of the metal basket.

By using this design, you give your visitors a convenient way of charging and to extend your warm welcome.

Ladder Shelf

Supplies:
Ladder
Pine wood
L-brackets
Drill
Screw

Instructions:
Cut the pinewood into incremental sizes. Decide how long you want the boards to be.
Put the ladder in place where you want it to stay, and stand it up.

Slide the boards you have made into the cross beams of the ladder, making sure the sizes are staggering as you go up.

Press the L-brackets up against the plank and the ladder cross beam. Secure the L-brackets using the drill.

Fill up the shelves with your favourite items. Bring organization and symmetry to your clutter.

Hexagonal Shelf

Supplies:

1 inch by 4 inch or 6 inch by 6-foot wood

Mitre saw (if you can't get the wood already cut at the hardware store)

Wood glue

Sandpaper

Sponge brush

Staple gun

Minimax wood finish in Natural

Acrylic paint of your choice

Instructions:

If you are cutting the wood yourself, set your mitre saw to 30 degrees. Cut six pieces of 8-inch pieces of wood. Make sure that the cuts on both sizes are angling inward.

Glue all the joints together using the wood glue to form a hexagon. Allow to dry the hexagon for at least an hour.

On the back side of the hexagon, staple each joint together with two staples. Allow to dry for at least 24 hours or overnight.

Once completely dry, sand out the uneven corners.

Paint the hexagon, or finish with a natural wax or varnish for a more rustic and organic look.

Use a bracket to hang each hexagonal shelf to the wall. You may also conceal hammer nails in the corner of each hexagon.

Place your favourite items inside the hexagon shelf. Use it to keep items in your living space clutter-free.

Chapter 7 - DIY Projects for Decluttering your Bedroom

The bedroom is your personal space. However small or large your house may be, the bedroom is a specific area in the house that's yours. It holds most of your personal stuff, such as clothes, shoes, books and so forth. It is where you sleep, recharge, and recuperate from the day's busy schedule, so it needs to be a relaxing room that's free from stressful clutter and mess. Despite the many things it contains, it should be organized properly so that the amount of stuff is not inundating. Organization puts things in order. It deals with clutter in a creative way, so that your bedroom does not just serve its function for sleeping, but it also looks good.

Sometimes a room is shared by more than one; and in which case, the occupants should have a means to provide each other with a space to call his own. The challenge to keep a bedroom organized is bigger when you share it with someone. Space becomes scant and boundaries will have to be set. This is where your creativity will come in. Use the following crafty ideas to solve your clutter problems.

Game Board Work of Art

Do you love game boards? Game boards are fun to play with and if you are an avid collector, they're quite fun to have. Unfortunately, game boards are bulky so they take up a lot of space. You don't really use them every day, so they tend to collect dust in the room. Turning your game boards into works of art will solve the whole issue about them being bulky.

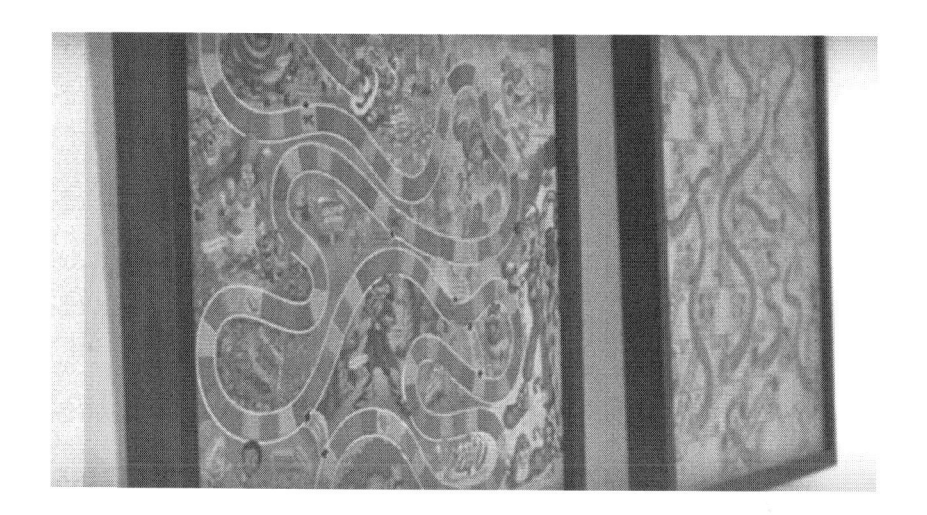

Supplies:
Gameboards
Blank frames or loose pieces of wood
Hooks and screws
Resealable bag (Ziploc)
Paint (optional)
Drill

Instructions:
Gather all your game boards. Measure the actual board and set aside the loose pieces (dice, playing pieces, money, etc.)
Frame each board, as if it's a photo or painting. If you cannot find a frame of the right size, create frames for each board. Paint the frames/wood in the same color, to give them a uniform look.
Decide on how you will hang them, then drill and attach hooks on the walls.
Contain the loose pieces of one Ziploc each and stick the bags at the back of their respective game board.

This game board work of art gives your bedroom a cool "game theme" and it solves the issue of clutter and mess in the most innovative way.

Hidden Controls

Do you always go around the house looking for the remote control? You want to lower down the volume on the screaming television, but you do it because the remote control is nowhere to be found. The hidden controls design makes use of Velcro so that you can store each remote in their proper places (and they are hidden conveniently) so they do not clutter your bedroom.

Supplies:

Velcro
Double-sided tape
Scissors

Instructions:

Decide where you want to "hide" your remote controls. Their best placed near your bed, so that you have easy access to it; but you can also have it near the actual machine (television, video player, etc.) Attach one side of the Velcro on the hidden area you've chosen and attach the opposite side of the Velcro to the remote control.

The small things your own are not messy but when there too much of them, they pile up to clutter the room. If you can conveniently hide them, so that you can pretend they don't exist, they don't have to clutter the room.

Toys in a Basket

Toys are lovely, but if you do not have a perfect place to put them away to, they can create such a messy pile in the room. This is most especially true if you have lots of stuffed toys lying around. You do not have to remove them; you just need a creative way to store them.

Supplies:

Metal rack
Drill and screws
Paint (optional)

Instructions:
Find an unused metal rack in the house or buy some in your local home depot. If necessary, paint the racks to achieve your aesthetic vision.
Bolt the racks on the wall. Decide if you want it to be low enough so that your child can reach it conveniently or high enough so that he or she will have a hard time getting to it.
Place the stuffed toys in the rack. Stack them closely so that it looks like they are cramped, but make sure that they appear looking out and standing up. Like they are inside a cage crying, "Please get me out of here!"

This storage idea also serves a decorative purpose. You do not just build a place to contain the toys, you also allow them to look cute in the room.

Makeup Magnet Board

This is another good use of magnets, this time for your precious makeup collection. By using a frame, you can showcase your daily stash so that they you have easy access to them, and they look absolutely prettier this way—standing on your desk like a work of art.

Supplies:
Empty picture frame
Metal sheet (magnetic)
Magnets
Double-sided tape
Plastic glass/cup

Instructions:
Remove the glass covering of the frame
Cover the open face of the frame with a metal sheet. Make sure that this sheet is magnetic.
Attach magnets to the backside of every makeup item you currently use. You can buy magnetic tapes with a "sticky" side but if you cannot find one of those, simply use double-sided tape at attach them to the makeup.
Get an empty glass and attach a magnet to one side.
Arrange your makeup on the frame. All your brushes and pencils will go in the glass. Arrange the other items all over the frame, as if you are scrapbooking.

Makeup allows women to turn their faces into true works of art. The most experienced makeup artists can make amazing transformations that can be likened to valuable masterpieces in the world of the arts. There are 2 designs for you. The second one covers the metal sheet with a decorated paper, so you can have a pretty board (aside from it being functional).

Arts and Crafts Wall

If you are into arts and crafts and you do a lot of work in your room, you need to have a perfect way to organize all your crafting materials. This design is fairly straightforward but if you execute it properly, you are going to transform your craft area into a legit work area.

Supplies:
Peg board
Hooks
Metal rod
Metal racks/baskets
Metal tin cans
Paint and brush (optional)

Instructions:
Bolt the peg board on the wall. You may paint on the peg board, so that you can give it some character, but you can leave it as raw and simple.
Hang a thin metal rod throughout the length of the wall. Make sure the rod is thin enough to accommodate spools of decorative tape, yarn, ribbon, etc.
Hang racks/baskets to contain your glitters, glitter glue, paint tubs, and so forth.
On the tin cans, organize your sharpie pens, colored pencils, paint brushes, and so forth.
Hang hooks and on them, you may hang your craft scissors

This design is going to make your function more efficient—and probably, more fun. Because who wouldn't have fun working in this area, right?

Bedside Table Charging Station

The bedside table is quite useful for the many personal things you have. And since there is a drawer, it gives you the opportunity to hide all kinds of messes, from plain sight. But decluttering is not just merely hiding things. The most effective decluttering work is creative and crafty. This design makes your charging station, conveniently hidden.

Supplies:
Extension cord
Drill
Double-sided tape

Instructions:
Position an extension cord inside your bedside drawer. You may need to drill a hole, to fit the cords, if you cannot simply slide it to the back. Securely tape the extension cord.
Start charging.

This design is simple, cheap, but sincerely convenient. It still leaves enough space for other things you have, such as a book, nightly medications, and so forth.

Folding is the Trick

The drawers are always messy because when you organize your clothes in the traditional ways, on top of each other, you end up messing the whole drawer when you get one thing. This folding trick helps to increase visualization and makes it easier for you to see everything the moment you open your drawer.

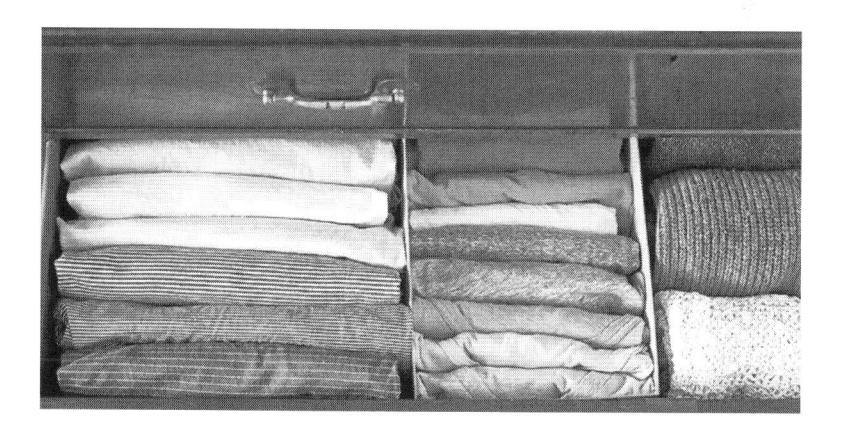

Supplies:
Boxes/cardboard

Instructions:
Get boxes that will serve as partitions for your drawer. If you do not have boxes an do not want to buy some, you can easily use shoe boxes for this. You can also use cardboards—just make sure they are sturdy enough to maintain the borders.

Neatly roll and fold your clothes and arrange them properly in their respective places. It's best to keep similar materials together so they are more or less the same size—cotton shirts, shorts, sweaters, underwear, and so forth.

Of course, this looks pretty in the picture, and it will demand so much from you, to be able to maintain this pretty picture, at all times.

Hooked on Scarves

If you have a lot of scarves, and you want to organize them in your closet, this is a simple but effective way to keep your scarves in order. You can do this at the back of the bedroom door, behind the cabinet door, or on any empty wall in your room.

Supplies:
Decorative hooks
Drill and screws/double-sided tape

Instructions:

Bolt the hooks you have on the surface that you've chosen

Arrange the scarves on the hooks—making sure that you can easily see every design from where they're hanging.

You can arrange your scarves by color or design, so that it looks organized, even in terms of aesthetic.

Roll Them Up

Here's a creative way to keep your jeans in order. Jeans take up a lot of space but by using this cabinet organizer, you can truly save precious space.

Supplies:
Cabinet organizer

Instructions:

Hang your cabinet organizer

Gather all your jeans and pants. You can also do the same thing to your leggings.

Roll them like a burrito and stick them into the slots

You can arrange your jeans, pants and leggings by color so that it does not just look neat, it also looks pretty. More importantly, with this design, it is definitely easier for you to get them out for you to wear.

Hanging Belts

Belts are best hung on your closet and here is a good way to do just that. You can install this design on any empty surface you have in the room—behind the door, behind the cabinet door, or any free wall space.

Supplies:

Metal rod
Curtain hooks (metal)
Drill and screws

Instructions:
Bolt the rod onto the surface you want to use
Hang the hooks throughout the length of the metal rod
Hang your belts

If you're a belt person this is the best way for you to showcase your collection. It's going give your closet some character.

Stacking Bras

This picture shows an organized underwear drawer but zoom in on the bras. This is simple, but it's aesthetically worth it, if you organize your bras this way because it saves space and makes it so much easier for you to get to the bra that you want to wear for the day.

Supplies:

Plastic trays/boxes

Instructions:
In a box or tray, simply lay your bras on top of each other.
Arrange the different boxes in the drawer, along with the panties.

Sometimes it's all about making practical moves that absolutely makes sense. This design is fairly simple, but it works.

Tension Rod Shoe Rack

If you do not have a shoe rack but you want to have one that's easy to create, using the least amount of materials and the least amount of money, this is the design you need. It makes use of a few tension rods. It's simple and is so useful.

Supplies:

Tension rods

Instructions:
Get yourself some tension rods. These are the rods you use to hang shower curtains. You need 2 rods per level/row, so you can securely lay your shoes on top of them.
Prepare the rods, a row-at-a-time, and make sure that they're secure before you lay your shoes on top of them.

Keep the boots at the very bottom, because they are heavy, and lay your flats and sandals on the higher levels. This is a very affordable shoe rack that's conveniently "portable", so you can keep moving them if you need to.

The Velcro Wall of Polish

Do you own a lot of nail polish? Nail polish is fun and playful, especially if you have them in nice bright colors, so it's really nice be able to showcase them. This "wall design" is going to absolutely give a pop of colors in your room and it will make it easy for you grab any bottle when you need one.

Supplies:

Velcro
Double-sided tape

Instructions:

Attach one side of the hard part of the Velcro onto the wall. You may cut small strips or you may transform the wall into a large Velcro contraption.
Get your nail polish and install the soft side of the Velcro on one surface of the nail polish.
Stick each bottle of nail polish in different directions.

This design is simple and creative. If you have a massive collection, your wall is going to look absolutely fantastic.

Cord Tubes

Cords of various gadgets and equipment can be a little messy. They look messy and they're bulky, but it's not like you can just remove them to take them out of the way. What you can do is to think of a creative way to keep them "together" so they do not look so bothersome. This cord tubes idea is absolutely cheap and easy to make, but it does so much for the messy cords.

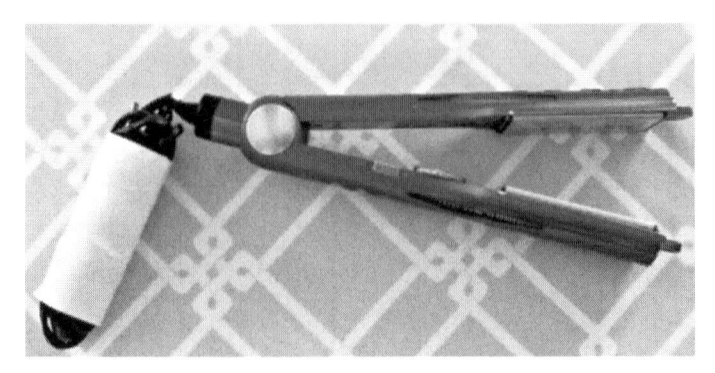

Supplies:

Tissue cores
Craft materials (optional)

Instructions:
Collect enough tissue cores and paper towel cores. You may choose to decorate the cores or simply reinforce them, so they become sturdier; but you can keep them simple and raw.
Fold the cords and carefully insert it into the cores

This idea will work for all kinds of gadgets such as the air conditioner, the television, and so forth. Who said you need to buy an expensive tool to keep your cords organized? You have so much material lying around in the house.

Clip Labels

Do you want to give your closet some order? Labelling your closet keeps everything in its proper place, and all you need are metal clips.

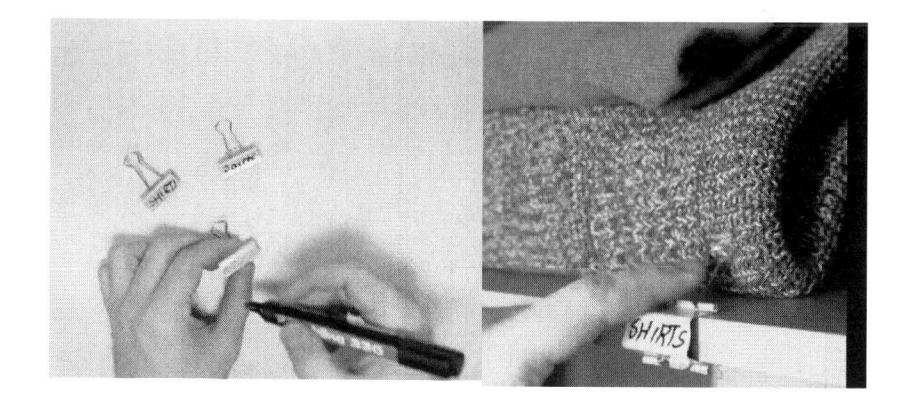

Supplies:
Metal clips
Sharpie pen

Instructions:
Determine where you want to put everything in your cabinet. Make sure to allocate enough space for the certain amount of clothing you have

On a metal clip, write the labels you wish to put on the inner part. You can use any colour of metal clip to match your aesthetic needs

Fix your cabinet and organize your clothes so that they are in their proper places

This idea is simple, but it works mostly because it's very easy to maintain. Organizing demands commitment. It's all nice in the beginning but you can easily mess it if you cannot keep it up.

Grooming Organizer

The desk organizer seems to be one of the most versatile supplies in the world because here you have a desk organizer holding your collection of grooming accessories. You have makeup brushes, hair dryer, flat iron; and if you choose a messed one, you can use it as an earring holder.

Supplies:
Desk organizer

Instructions:
Get yourself a desk organizer and as much as possible, try to find a metal mesh kind, so that you can use it as an earring organizer too. Put everything in place. Any grooming tool you are using. Arrange them in such a way, so that you can get to any of them, easily.

This idea keeps your stuff together so they are not making a mess on your table. It turns a simple desk organizer that usually holds paper, into something that holds a number of your grooming tools.

Storage Bed

In the bedroom, the bed is the most important furniture you need, but you also need storage. Whether it's going to store your clothes or other things, you need it. When you have little space to work with, you need to be a little creative. This bed design is not only a space saver; it is a good solution for unwanted clutter. If you have lots of that and you want a place to put them away into, the drawers will do a brilliant job.

Supplies:
Wood
Wood saw
Hammer and nails
Sandpaper
Paint
Mattress

Instructions:

The size of your cabinet/bed frame will be determined by the size of your mattress. You need to prepare a lot of wood to build this. You need a large enough sheet of wood that's as big as the mattress, and it should be strong enough to function as the roof of the bed frame or platform. You also need four rectangular sheets to form the sides of the frame; and another wooden sheet as big as the roof, to form the floor of the bed or the cabinet/storage.

Determine the size and number of drawers you want to install on your bed frame so you can prepare the wood for the drawers. You need to prepare the sides, the back the front, and the floor of each drawer. In lieu of a bed frame, you may just cut a notch from the front wall, so that functions as a drawer handle.

Assemble each drawer with wood glue, and reinforce each one of them with nails. Assemble the bed frame and make sure that its construction is strong and stable to carry weight and force. Cut slots on the bed frame to fit the drawers. To add stability to the frame, you may build walls to support each drawer.

Sand the wood and paint it. Make sure that the entire structure is secure.

Lay the mattress on your new bed frame.

This obviously requires some technical skill. If you are not well equipped in the carpentry department, you may take this design to an expert, and have them build this for you.

Wire Mesh Display

Here is a wall installation that's quite simple, but it offers both functional and decorative value.

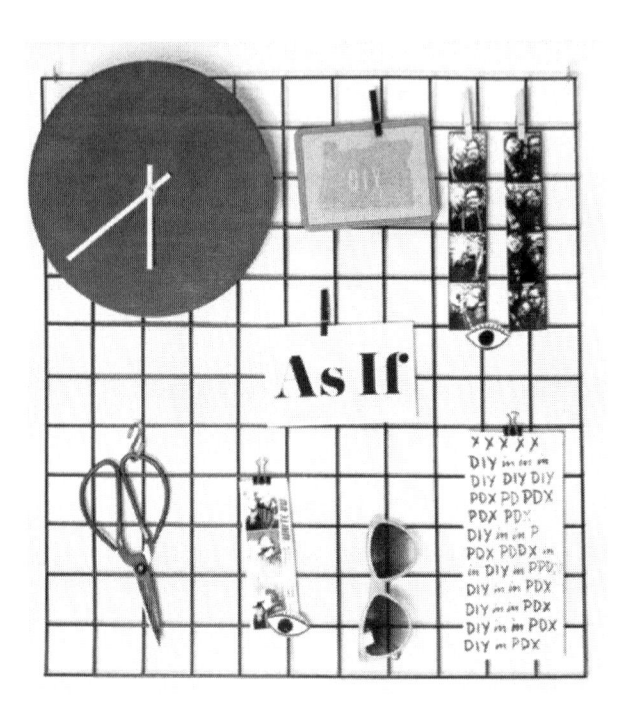

Supplies:
Wire mesh
Metal clips
Wooden clips
Hooks
Wall clock
Paint and brush (optional)

Instructions:

Paint the wire mesh in your desired color. You may also leave it in its original color if you wish to keep things raw.

Bolt the mesh to the wall with a screw. Make sure that it is secure.

Attach the different types of clips and hooks to the wire mesh. Decide on what you want to put on the wire mesh. You can put photos, receipts, notes, and other important things. You can even hang accessories and jewelry.

Attach a wall clock onto the wire mesh. A small one would be best so that it's not too heavy.

Most people use a blackboard or a corkboard for the same function, but this is a cool idea that allows you to attach even more things.

Leather Mail Pouches

Here's a simple mailbox design that you can create for your bedroom. The leather gives it a sophisticated feel and adds to the aesthetic of your private space.

Supplies:
Wooden sheet
Leather
Stapler
Sandpaper
Wood varnish and brush

Instructions:
Cut a rectangular sheet of wood to your desired size. Sand it to make it smooth and apply varnish to it/
Cut sheets of leather to form the pouches. Make sure that it is large enough to hold your mail.
Create the leather pouches by stapling the leather sheets to the wood. Brown is the staple color, but you can use any color of leather if you want.

This can also be a worthy addition to your study to help you keep everything neat and tidy.

Pullout Drawer Under the Bed

The area under the bed is a lot of wasted space. If you want to add storage in your bedroom to effectively deal with the clutter you have lying around, you can simply add drawers under your bed. This takes almost zero carpentry skill, unlike the previous bed design. This works on any existing bed that you have and old drawers that you are no longer using. Instead of throwing old drawers away, you can give them a new function, as under-the-bed storage.

Supplies:
Old drawer
Paint and brush (optional)
Cabinet handle or knob (optional)
Wheels (4)

Instructions:
Find an old drawer that's lying around the house. If you can't find one you will have to construct one, so that will require for you to gather some wooden sheets to assemble into drawers or boxes. If you do not want to create a drawer, you can also use a wooden crate.

If the existing drawer has good paint, you can leave it, as is. But if you think it needs some retouch, you can give it a fresh layer of paint to match your bed and your bedroom. You may or may not change the drawer handle—it's really up to you.

Attach wheels to the bottom of the drawer. The wheels will make it easier for you to pull the drawer out from under the bed, regardless of the load it is carrying.

The beauty of this storage space is that it utilizes space that you are probably not even using.

Bedside Pockets

Here's a good way to utilize the side of your beds. If you want to create extra storage, in lieu of a bulky bedside table, you can have this instead. A bedside pocket can contain all kinds of things—books, stuffed toys, and other things. You can use used clothing or scarves for the cloth, so you do not have to spend extra money for fabric.

Supplies:
Fabric
Needle and thread
Thin foam (optional)

Instructions:

Cut scraps of cloth in different designs that more or less go with each other; these will become the pouches or pockets. Also prepare a thin sheet of cloth for piping (or the edges). Cut a large piece of cloth that will be the back—this will be the part of the bedside pockets that you will tuck in with the mattress.

Sew the small pouches on the large cloth, to form the individual pockets. Secure the edges with piping so that the stitches won't just come lose.

If you wish to make the pockets sturdy, you can sandwich a thin layer of foam between two pieces of cloth or you can insert some kind of cardboard. You can also think of securing the pocket in between the bed and the mattress, with a ribbon or string.

Upside Down Bookcase

By virtue of gravity, everything that's up will go down, so why aren't the books falling down? Well, before you find out how it does, let's first highlight the usefulness of this design. A single shelf only has one surface, but this design allows you to put things on top and books at the bottom. Now are you ready to find out how to make one?

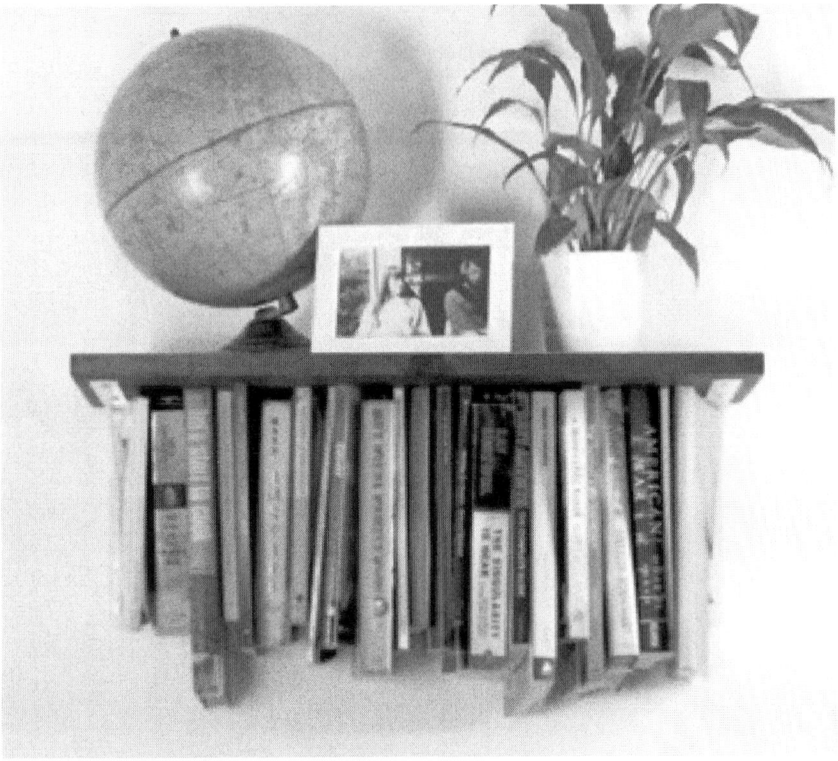

Supplies:
Wooden plank or sheet
Wood saw
Wood varnish and brush
Sandpaper
Thick garter or rubber
Stapler
Drill and screws

Instructions:

Determine what length of a self you want and need in your room. Prepare the wood. Sand the edges, until they're smooth, and apply varnish to the surface to make it look very clean.

Turn the wood around and attach the garters to the bottom of the shelf. To make sure that it will securely hold each book, you need to make the garter short so that even when the book is inserted, it is going to tightly hold the item. Carefully attach each one with a stapler. You may practice tugging on the garters, to make sure the attachment is strong enough before you use it.

Bolt the shelf to the wall, using a screw. You may use a wall bracket if you want to reinforce the strength.

Just make sure that the garter or rubber that you use is taut and thick enough so it doesn't sag. This design is also going to work for office and living room bookshelves.

Wall of Makeup and Stuff

These acrylic cases are often used in craft rooms, to hold art materials. Have you ever thought of using these cases for your makeup? If you cannot find these cases anywhere, you can buy acrylic sheets that will allow you to build one of these, or you can use wood instead.

Supplies:
Acrylic sheets
Acrylic glue
Drill and screws

Instructions:
Design the acrylic cases based on what you plan to put in them. Look at the bulk of your makeup and other products, so you know how many shelves you need to make for the case.
Cut the acrylic according to the measurements you obtain. You need one large square or rectangular one to form the back of the case. You also need three rectangular ones to form the outer frame of the case and two rectangular acrylic pieces for every shelf layer you are going to have.
Assemble the case by gluing the acrylic pieces together. Make sure it is secure, so that it can hold everything in place.
Bolt the cases to the wall and make sure it is strong enough.

Arrange your make up, perfume, lotions, nail polish and other personal grooming products on the case.

This is best placed by the mirror, where you usually apply your makeup.

Glasses on Hangers

Here is an interesting idea that will save you space and get rid of the bulky cases.

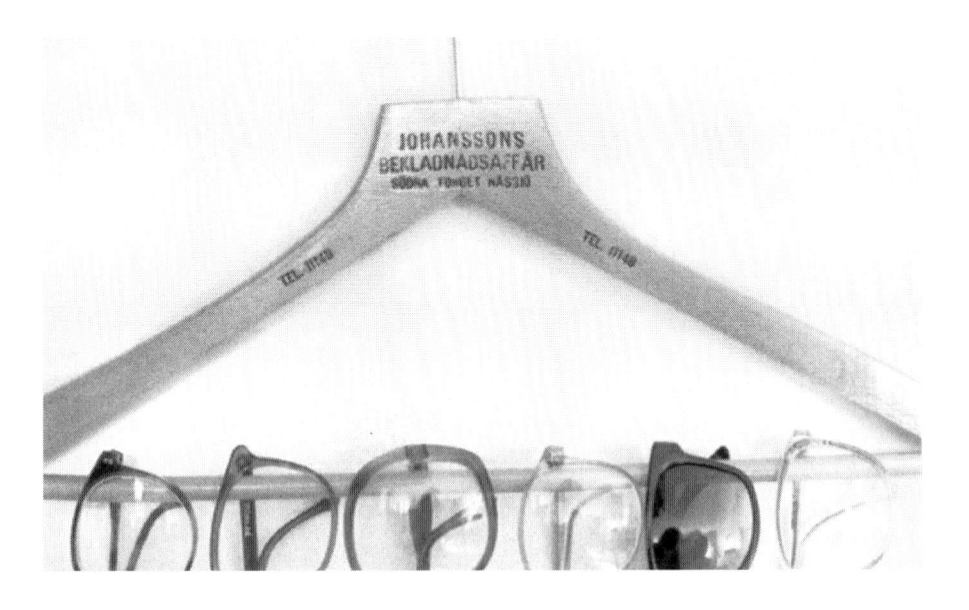

Supplies:
Clothes hanger
Paint and brush (optional)

Instructions:

Find an unused clothes hanger. As this is going to function more than a clothes hanger, it's good if you can choose a nice-looking hanger, especially if you're going to have it out and displayed. You may or may not choose to paint it a different color, but you can keep it in it raw.

Bolt the hanger to the wall. Arrange the eyeglasses on the hanger.

Hook, Line and Scarves

Here is a simple idea for your scarves, hoods, and bonnets. This design keeps things in great order. You don't have to ransack your closet anymore just to pull out the one that you need, and it's easy to see everything.

Supplies:
Wall bracket
Rubberized rope
Shower curtain rings
Drill and screw

Instructions:

To determine the length of the rope you need to install and the position of the wall brackets, you need to count how many things you are going to hang. Of course, affording length means you do not have to make adjustments in the future, if your collection increases in number. Basically, you should not shy away where length is concerned because that will mean more space.

Bolt the brackets to the wall and attach the ropes to these brackets. Attach the hooks on the rope and arrange the scarves, hoods, and bonnets on them.

Color-coded Closet

This is a simple idea. If you want your closet to look clean and organized at all times, you have to follow a system when you arrange your clothes. Color-coding is a very important thing when you're after order and uniformity. Mixing colors cause visual chaos; arranging the clothes by similar color will bring some order to the overall appearance of your closet.

Supplies:
Hangers

Instructions:
Obtain hangers. Make sure the hangers are of the same color, type and brand. In other words, you should use identical hangers so they are of the same color, size, shape and form.
Gather your clothes (mostly shirts, dresses and blouses that you have to hang) and group them together according to color.
Hang the clothes by color, but as you do, make sure that the hangers face the same away. This will give the closet a very neat appearance that goes beyond color coding and similar hangers.

Necklace Stand

Maybe you have a number of necklaces and you wish to give a perfect place for them. Here is a simple design and it involves some craft work if you are up for it. Instead of getting them tangled in boxes, you can hang them so that they are accessible and visually appealing.

Supplies:
Wooden rod
T-shaped wooden rod holder
Flat wooden cylinder
Wood glue
Metallic spray paint

Instructions
Prepare the wooden rods that will form the body of this design. You need a long one that will form the legs or length; and you will need two short ones that will form the width or the arms of the design.
Prepare the flat cylinder wooden piece. This will base of the whole stand, so it should be sturdy and wide enough to balance the weight of the design. Punch hole in the middle, so that it will fit the circumference of the rods.
Paint all the pieces using metallic spray paint. Choose metallic because it will give it a sophisticated look—fitting for your jewelry, whether or not they are expensive.
Assemble the different pieces together. You may apply wood glue to secure everything in place.
Arrange your necklaces on the "arms" of the necklace holder. Make sure there is enough space between each one of them.

If you think this design is not enough to hold all the necklaces you own, you can install multiple levels of arms throughout the height of the stand. This will allow you to hang more necklaces without making more than one stand.

Bags Inside a Bag

Are you having a hard time containing the bags you own? Bags are bulky and their size and shape is so random that it's so hard to really keep them organized. They will take a lot of space unless you become a little creative. Well, this idea will cost you nothing at all. All you need are your bags—that's it.

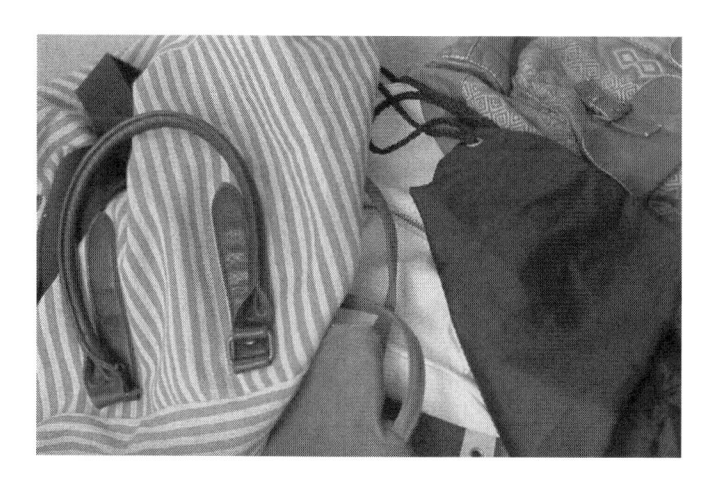

Supplies:
Bags

Instructions:
Gather all your bags. Group them into two—hard leather bags and soft cotton or cloth bags.
How this works is that you put smaller bags into bigger bags so that in the end, you will only have one large bag left. In the case of hard leather bags, however, you cannot really put them inside another hard bag so smaller and softer bags will basically go inside these larger and harder bags.

After properly containing the smaller bags into the bigger ones, you will need a place to contain the big ones. Of course, there are a few ideas for these. You can hang them on coat rack or on hooks. You can also put them in boxes or crates.

Hanging Crates

Crates and boxes make very good containers because they're very spacious. This idea organizes all the crates, so that it doesn't take up much space. It hangs from the ceiling—in the corner of the room—which is basically under-utilized space.

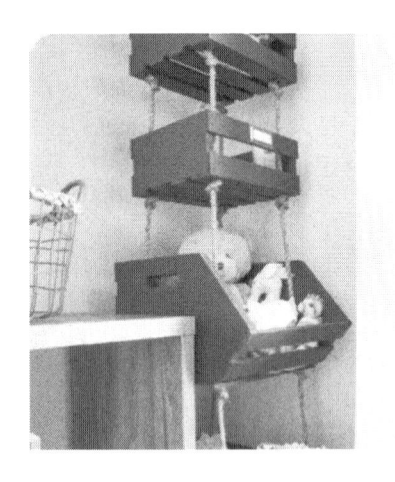

Supplies:
Wooden crates
Rope
Paint and brush

Instructions:

Obtain different sizes and forms of wooden crates. You don't really need to buy one. You may have crates lying around in the house—feel free to use them.

Decide what color you want your crates to be. It can be any color that matches your room. Punch a hole through the crates so that you can string the rope from ceiling to floor.

Hang the rope to the ceiling. You will need about four long pieces of rope because it is supposed to hold the crates on four corners. Allow these ropes to be long because you have to make allowance for the knots that you will put at the bottom of each crate.

Arrange the crates into position—one on top of each other. String the rope through and create a knot at the bottom of each crate, to secure it.

The space you create with this extra storage is going to be valuable. You can put all kinds of things on the crate. You can put toys, bags, linens, and so forth. Instead of keeping things cramped in the closet, you can utilize the area in the corner of the room, and that will have things rather organized.

Convertible Desk/Shelf

If you do some work in the bedroom you need a workspace. But if you do not really have so much space to house a real desk, you can apply this clever design. It's a shelf that converts to a desk. When not in use, it can hold your books and whatnot; and with one swift move, you can transform it a desk, so that you can work on it.

Supplies:
Wood
Wood saw
Wood glue
Sandpaper
Paint and brush
Hinge
Drill and screws

Instructions:
Prepare the wood according to the size of shelf/desk you wish to have. You will need to assemble two intricately crafted pieces that will form the top and bottom parts of the shelf. You'll need two large rectangular pieces which will form the top and bottom. You'll need two more pieces that are rather of the same size, except that it is shorter in width. To construct the sides of the shelf, you initially need to cut smaller rectangular piece of wood. Cut it diagonally, and on the top piece, carve out a circle—this should leave a notch on the bottom piece. Assemble the two large pieces by bringing everything together with wood glue. You may secure it with nails.

Apply a hinge mechanism on the sides that will connect the top and bottom pieces. This will permit the transformation from shelf to desk. Run sandpaper through the whole structure, and make sure it is smooth. Apply paint, using a color of your choice. It is nice to paint of the same color as the wall, so it would blend.
Bolt the desk at the bottom part of the desk, leaving the top part the movable part of this whole design.

When you need to work, you just have to pull a chair and your desk ought to be ready for use. It's a very useful design and it doesn't take a carpenter to get this done.

Bunch of Headbands

Headbands are pretty but they can appear quite messy if they're not arranged neatly. This design is nice because it makes it easy for you to view the collection and pick one easily.

Supplies:
Tension rods
Cylinder shaped foam
Decorative paper/tape

Instructions:
Take foam cylinders that are wide enough to hold the regular size of headbands. If you cannot find one, you may need to construct one using a cardboard. As soon as this cylinder is formed, you should decorate it with colored paper and tape.

Attach the cylinder onto a tension rod and lay it on the drawer. Make sure it is secure.

Arrange the different headbands along the length of the cylinder.

The design is fairly straightforward, and it gives the pretty little things a proper place.

Drawer Organizer

You may have small things like clips, ribbons, hair ties, and all kinds of things lying around in the room. Perhaps it usually litters your drawer; you can now restore some order by getting an organizer. Some of the organizers come in multiple dividers. More compartments mean you can put more things in them.

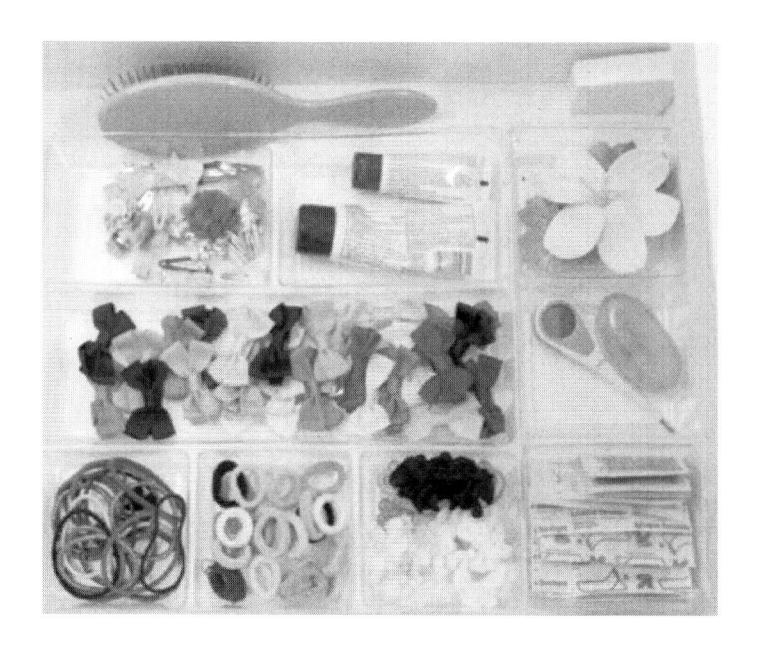

Supplies:
Desk organizer

Instructions:
Find for yourself a nice desk organizer. It should perfectly fit into your drawer; and as much as you can, you should try maximize the use of any space you have so if you need to put more containers in a single drawer, then you should.
Decide on what you're going to put into the different compartments. Group them together and arrange them into the different compartments. You may even label them, if you want, although that is not necessary.

Hanging Hats

This idea of using clips keeps your hats safe on the wall, while simultaneously looking like fancy décor.

Supplies:
Wooden clips
Glue

Instructions:
Arrange each wooden clip on the wall and glue them securely
Arrange your hat collection. One clip for a hat, unless it's quite heavy, in which case you may need two clips to hold it.

Earring Box

This box allows you to hold the earrings in a fashion that perfectly displays them. You can display the pairs beside each other, so they can look pretty together.

Supplies:
Box
Foam sheets
Glue

Instructions:
Find yourself a nice box. It should be big enough to fit all your earrings, but it should be small enough to be dainty. If you can find a box that's already decorated, that's good, but you may need have to do some decorating if you cannot find a beautiful box.
Obtain a foam sheet. Cut rectangular sheets of the foam and roll it into a cylinder. The cylinders ought to be of the length the same as the box

so that when you lay them beside each other—it will snugly fit into the box.

Lay the rolled foam sheets on the box beside each other. You may glue the cylinders to the bottom of the box to secure it in place.

Arrange the earrings on the box, by pairs.

Jewelry boxes are fancy things and this is such an elegant and dainty way to keep them organized. This design is also good for rings. You can even mix both rings and earring in a single case, but make sure that you give them enough space between each pair, so that it does not look too cramped.

Neck Tie Hanger

If you own quite a number of neckties, here is a cool idea that will allow you to properly showcase your collection and save a lot of space.

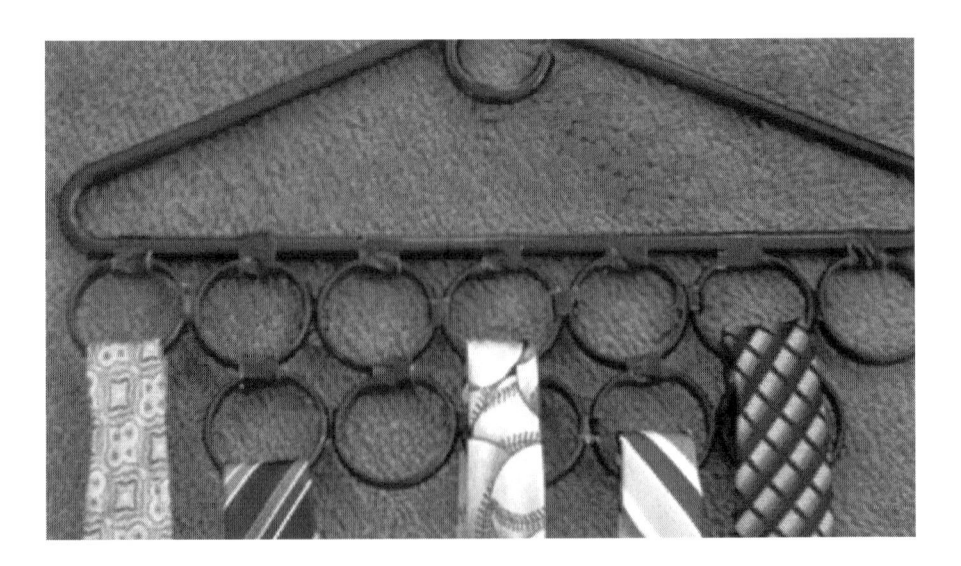

Supplies:
Hanger
Shower curtain rings
Tape
Paint and brush (optional)

Instructions:
Find yourself a hanger. Any hanger will do.
Obtain a number of shower curtain rings and arrange them on the hanger using tape. If you're going to use a black hanger, you ought to use black shower curtain rings, and black electrical tape. This will keep the colors solid.
Arrange the neckties, one for each ring. If you need to create multiple levels (more than one, in fact) you should do so, in order to maximize the use of the hanger.

Storage Beneath the Seat

It's usual to convert chairs to storage, but why should you limit yourself? This design creates extra storage space, so you can hide more clutter.

Supplies:
Wood
Sandpaper
Foam/cushion
Wood saw
Paint and brush
Cloth
Hinge and screw
Hammer and nails

Instructions:
Prepare the different pieces of wood. You'll need four rectangular blocks of wood, long enough to form the legs of the chair, four flat rectangular sheets to form the walls of the storage area/seat, two square sheets to form the roof and the floor of the storage/seat, two thick rectangular pieces of wood to form the back of the chair. You have this piece at an angle, depending on the design you wish to achieve.

Assemble the different pieces of wood to build the chair. Secure every piece with nails. You cannot have a chair that will break into pieces when you sit down.

Build the seat or cushion, which is also to be the cover of the chair storage. Fix the cushion or foam on the wood and cover it with your chosen fabric. Attach the cushion to the wood.

Attach the seat/cover to the char using a hinge so that it opens conveniently on one side.

Stuffed Toy Zoo

Here's a very creative idea for your stuffed animals. Instead of allowing them to get lost in the wild, it is best when you can keep them in the cage because not only will keep things organized, it also gives the children a perfect place to put away their toys. The idea is fairly straightforward but it works beautifully in any kid's room.

Supplies:
Wood
Wood saw
Sandpaper
Hammer and nails
Elastic rope
Paint and brush
Drill

Instructions:
1. Prepare the wood that you're going to use. You will need eight rectangular blocks to form the top and bottom of the cage; and you will need four longer rectangular blocks of wood that will form the corners of the cage.
2. Assemble the cage by bringing together the pieces. Form the top and the bottom part, first. As soon as you have everything formed, you need to bring the top and bottom parts together by attaching the wood that's meant to form the corners of the cage.
3. Drill holes through the width of the wood.
4. Sand the wood and paint it in your color of choice.
5. To form the cage bars, you need to slit the elastic rope from top to bottom and tie them at both ends.
6. Put the stuffed animals inside the cage. Make sure they face the front so they appear like real animals in the zoo.

Everyone enjoys a day at the zoo. You may or may not create alphabet blocks to spell the word ZOO or you may keep it as is. Sometimes it's possible to by ready-made block letters, so you do not have to sculpt your own.

Shoe Hanger

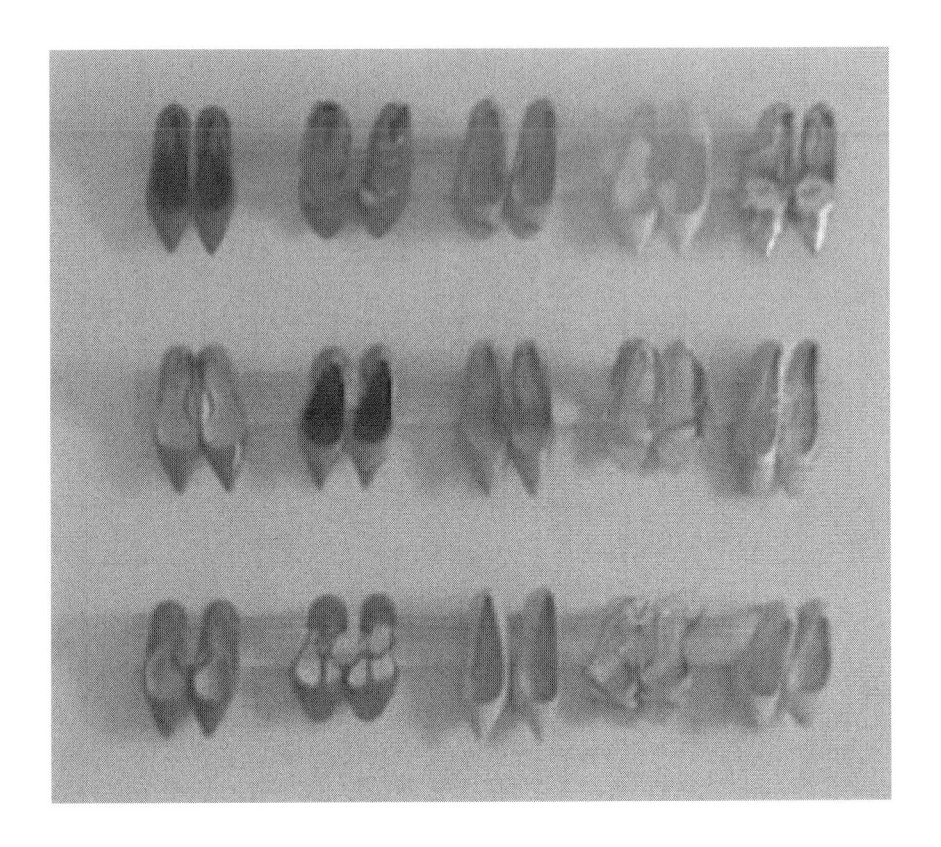

Supplies:
Crown moulding
Base moulding
Wood glue
Nail gun
Measuring tape
Screws
Drywall studs
High gloss paint with medium size paint brush

Instructions:

Measure out the desired length for your shoe rack. Cut each of the base moulding and crown moulding to length.

Using wood glue, attach the crown moulding to the base moulding. Make sure the angled ends are connecting each other.

Secure with a finishing nail and hammer or a nail gun.

Let dry before painting it to your desired colour.

Once dry, screw into wall studs using wood screws, or if it's drywall, insert drywall studs and screw into them.

Hang up your shoes and display!

Accessory Rack

Supplies:
Tension Rod

Instructions:
Adhere a tension rod in your closet, or an unused nook.
Place some S-hooks and use these to hang scarves or hats. Clasp jewelleries such as bracelets and necklaces onto the rod.

Boots hanger

Supplies:
Pants hanger
Pool noodles

Instructions:
Hang up boots using a pants hanger to keep pair together and free up some floor space. Long boots tend to end up all over the place when there is no support. Or, place cut-out pool noodles to size and insert them into each boot to keep them in shape.

Bedsheet Bundle

Supplies:
Pillowcase
Sheets (Fitted or Flat)
Duvet/Blanket Cover
Anything else that belongs to a bedsheet set

Instructions:
Spread the pillowcase flat. Fold in half, then once over.
Fold the fitted or flat sheet so that there is space on all four sides it can fit on the pillowcase.
Fold the duvet the same way as the fitted sheets.
Stack the duvet and sheets, one on top of another.
Move the neat and tidy stack of the pillowcase.
Unfold the pillowcase with the opening mouth facing toward you.
Stretch your arms taut through the pillowcase. Grab the right corner of the stack with your right hand. Use your left hand for the left corner of the stack.
While holding this stack inside the pillowcase, work it over your hands and onto the stack of linens.
Use your other hand to pull the pillowcase over the rest of the stack.
Fold the empty half or whatever space remains of the pillowcase and you're done.

Vertical Closet Space

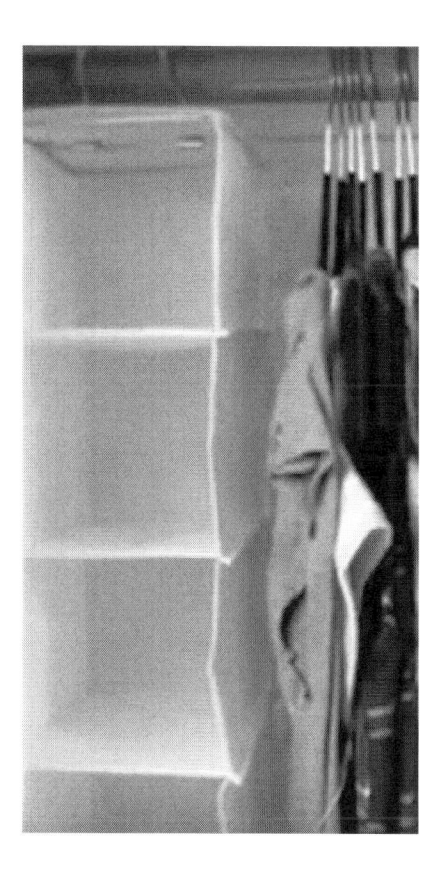

Supplies:
Hanging shelf

Instructions:
Save up on closet space by freeing some items. Get a vertical hanging storage shelf that is usually made of cloth. Place it inside your clothes hanging rod.
You can use the shelves to put small folded pieces of clothing such as shirts, scarves, underwear or socks.

Scarves hanger

Supplies:
Wooden Hanger
Pencil
Wax paper
Shower curtain rings or metal drapery
Needle nose pliers
Permanent adhesive
Permanent markers
Scissors

Hot glue gun
Several toothpicks
Thread or embroidery floss

Instructions:
Place hanger on wax paper and trace the shape of the hanger bottom. Set the hanger aside.
Using needle pliers (if needed), bend the clips off rings.
Aligning the rings on your tracing, arrange the rings in a row.
If desired, set the rest of the rings in place.
With a permanent marker, mark contact points on each ring.
Squeeze a small amount of permanent adhesive on wax paper.
Use toothpick to apply adhesive to marks on rings. Let the adhesive to dry cure for 10 minutes.
Once the adhesive is "cured", push the rings together so that each one will adhere to the other.
If necessary, apply more adhesive and do the same procedure for the rest of the rings.
Attach the rings to hanger after allowing the adhesive to cure for 24-48 hours. Be very careful not to disturb or move them now.
Option 1: Binding to Hanger
If you have a single row of rings, this is the preferred method to use. Add it as a decorative element to option 1 if you desire pops of colours.
Cut approximately 2 ½ yards of floss or thread.
Fold this thread in half, then fold in half again. Fold for a third time.
Wrap a loop end of the thread around the glued section of 2 rings.
Feed the other end of thread through this loop. To secure, pull tight the thread around the rings.

Wrap the thread around glued section until it ends on the backside of the rings. Secure this in place with a small dot of hot glue.

Do the same process for the rest of the rings until all rings are bound together.

Bind the rings to the hanger.

Hang your scarves through the loops or rings, then place the hanger inside your closet.

Wall Bins

Wall bins are great storage spaces because it makes use of space that is otherwise unutilized. By creating wall bins, it's like you're installing low-level cupboards for all kinds of clutter that you normally have lying around the house.

Supplies:
Crates
Drill and screws
Storage boxes
Paint and brush (optional)
Wood varnish (optional)

Instructions:
Decide if you want to repaint the crates that you obtained. If you want them to be a particular color, you may paint them; but if you want to achieve a more rustic appeal, you can leave them as is. If the crates are made of wood, you can decide to just give it a light varnish. This will make it easier for you to clean by wiping, if and when it collects dust. Bolt the crates onto the wall, with the bottom facing the surface. This will have the crates standing sideways, resembling the appearance of a shelf. You may arrange two to three crates on top of each other in a vertical orientation; or you may keep them beside each other, in a horizontal line. Make sure to provide enough screws to keep the crates in place. And make sure that the it's secure enough to hold the items you wish to store.
Place boxes into the crates on the wall. This will give you a very creative "drawer" of sorts to store your things in.

These wall bins may be installed in any room. They are best placed near the door, such as the one in your foyer, so that you can use it to keep things like your keys, gloves, scarves and whatnot. In the bathroom, this storage space can be for your clean towels or various grooming materials.

Personal Buckets

Everyone in the house has personal clutter to keep away. That's why you have wallets, keys, mobile phones, chargers and whatnot messily lying around in the house. Assigning personal buckets/baskets for every person in the house keeps the personal clutter in some kind of order. If you have a staircase in the living room, the lowest steps are best to use for this design.

Supplies:
Decorative baskets or buckets
Ribbons
Cardboard
Sharpie pen
Double-sided tape

Instructions:

Obtain decorative baskets or buckets. Make sure there is one basket or bucket for every person in the house

On pieces of cardboard, legibly and beautifully write the names of the people in the house.

Stick the names onto their assigned basket or bucket and decorate each one with a ribbon.

Position the buckets on the stairs in ascending order of age.

It is important that you instruct the people of the house as what they may or may not put into these baskets or buckets. Tell them they are "temporary storage" and not free space to accumulate junk.

Under the Staircase

If you want to maximize the function of every space in house, you will not overlook the area under the staircase. There's nothing else that you can put in there given the low vertical space, but you can convert it into cabinet space, where you can put all kinds of things, such as books, decorative items, albums, magazines and whatnot.

Supplies:
Carpenter's ruler and pencil
Wooden planks
Wooden saw
Nails and hammer
Wood glue
Sand paper
Paint/Wood varnish and brush (optional)

Instructions:
Plan the design you are going to follow, such a number of horizontal shelving and vertical partitions
Following the plan, you made, measure the wooden planks and cut them into the right dimensions
With wood glue and nails, bring the loose pieces of wooden planks together, to create shelves with vertical partitions, make sure every section is secure so it can safely contain anything you wish to put in it
Run sandpaper on the edges to make it smooth
You may keep it in its original color, to keep it raw; but you can also put paint or varnish over it

Shelving is very important if you want to keep clutter out of the way. The area under the stairs will make good shelving space because otherwise that's just going to be empty an unused. With this simple design, you significantly maximize storage space in the living room.

Wall Shelving

Utilizing the wall, for extra shelving, is always a good idea. You can install shelves in various areas in the living room—above the couch, beside the door, and so forth. This design is probably the simplest you can use and it can contain small items—mostly decorative in nature. But you can create all kinds of wall shelving, for all kinds of purposes.

Supplies:
Wooden planks
Wood glue
Sand paper
Wood varnish
Drill and screws

Instructions:
Determine what design you want to create for your wall shelf
Measure the wooden planks, depending on the design you wish to create

Assemble the frames or shelves using wood glue and make sure it dries securely

Run sand paper through it to give it a smooth surface

Apply wood varnish

Bolt the frames or shelves on the wall. Make sure it is secure before you use it

Option 2: Gluing to Hanger

If you have many rows of rings held together, this is the preferred method.

Line rings up to the hanger and mark contact points on both the hanger and the rings using a sharpie or marker. Dab a small amount of adhesive onto wax paper.

Using a toothpick, apply adhesive to the marks on rings and hanger. Allow the adhesive to cure for at least 10 minutes.

Push the rings and hanger together. Hold them in place until both bond well.

Clamp hanger and rings together and allow to cure for 24-48 hours.

Hang your scarves through the loops or rings, then place the hanger inside your closet.

The Ottoman Storage

An ottoman is a small chair or couch that does not have a back; and it has multiple uses: the obvious is that you sit on it, but you can also use it as a foot rest, and storage. This ottoman storage design is also a table—so you get more function for a single piece, making it absolutely amazing.

Supplies:
4 pcs square boards 40cm by 40cm
4 pcs boards 48cm by 44cm
Wood glue
Foam padding with fabric of your choice
Staples

Instructions:
Start with the 2 square boards. Using wood glue, attach a square of foam padding the same size.
Facing foam side down, place the square onto the fabric of your choice.
Turn in the sides of the fabric and staple into place to make tight fit cover.

Take the 2 pcs of 48cm by 44cm boards and glue the padded pieces to one of them.

Make an open box using the 44cm by 44cm boards, attaching each joint by gluing them.

Attach the remaining board that is 48cm by 44cm to form the bottom of the box, gluing and nailing this as well.

Stain the entire piece and let it dry.

Attach four sturdy casters to the bottom of the box you made, making sure to place one near each other.

Turn it over and place the padded section on top with plain side up, but do not nail it down.

You can now use the ottoman as a storage table for items that you prefer to hide and de-clutter, but keep. You can also flip to the side with the padded foam and make an extra seat for your guests, family, and friends. You may also make this ottoman rectangular in shape. Of course if you do that, the dimensions of the wooden pieces will be different. So make necessary adjustments.

Coffee table crate

Supplies:
4 wood crates
1 can of wood stain
1-piece heavy duty plywood
4 caster wheels with locks
Foam or paint brush for stain
24 5/8" wood screws
4 small L brackets
Electric wood sander

Instructions:

Using an electric wood sander, sand the edges of your wooden crates. This will this make the finished products look pleasing. It is also a safe option when you have toddlers or kids running around your home. You definitely don't want any sharp corners that may cause injuries.

Stain or paint your wood crates using a foam brush or a paint brush. For more control, you can choose to use a towel or a rag. Put at least two coats. Allow to dry completely before proceeding.

Wait for the paint/stain to be completely dry. Attach your caster wheels by screwing them to the bottom of your plywood.

Put your crates together on how you want them to come together. Drill them once you are happy and satisfied with your chosen arrangement.

Drill 4 screws at the bottom of each crate to the plywood.

Use a few more screws to hold the crates together. This will provide your coffee table much better stability.

Once you screw all four wooden crates together, measure the space between them. Cut a piece of plywood to fit.

Once you have measured this, cut out your plywood and stain it. Allow to dry completely.

Screw in your L-brackets. Put your piece of plywood in and enjoy your new coffee table. You can put loads of stuff and small items in the many nooks and crannies of this piece.

Labelled Organizers and Dividers

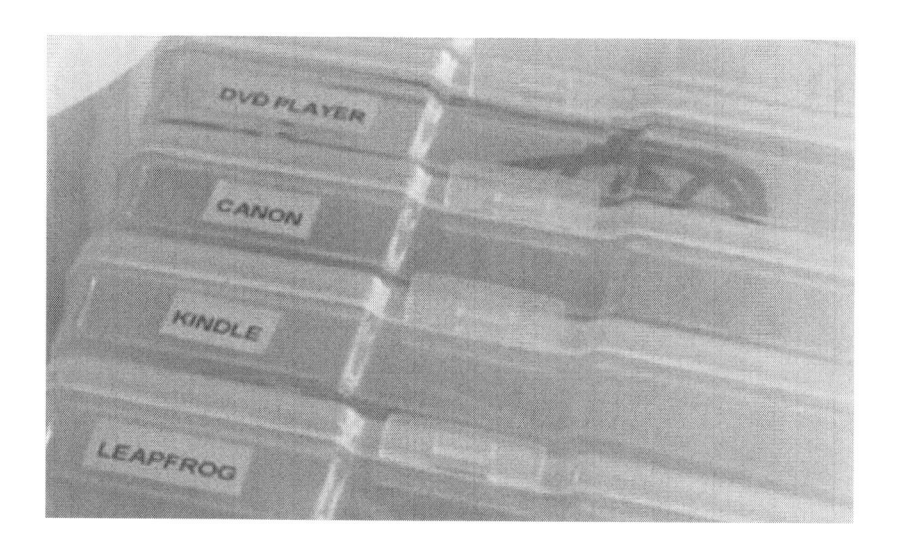

Supplies:
Clear organizers

Instructions:
You home office table can be a major source of clutter. Put some organization to your desk by sorting and placing a special house for each of them.

Get a bunch of clear organizers and place one or more items inside that belong to the same category.

On the outside of the container, near the opening, place a label to state what items are inside it. This can help you save time when you need to find what you need.

To-do list Memo Pad

Supplies:
Clipboard or corkboard
Paper or memo pads
Magnetic Strips

Instructions:
Cut magnetic strips according to the size of the clipboard or corkboard you will be putting up.
Make sure you cover the sides with the strips for the most support.
Take out the protective covering from the magnetic strips and plaster it on to a wall. If the wall isn't magnetic, you may place the same sized magnetic strips to stick your corkboard on. You may also use double sided foam tape or other strong tapes for this.
Place pieces of blank paper on to the clipboard. If using a corkboard, have some pins ready.
It is better to place this item at an area that is visible and accessible to you. If using it for your home office, have it in front of your workstation. This allows you to jot down important reminders. You can also have this in the kitchen as a grocery list reminder. That way, no one will keep forgetting what to put in the grocery list, and everyone is happy.

Magazine Rack Side table

Supplies:
Wooden magazine rack or file divider/folder
Drill bit
Screw

Instructions:
If there is extra space beside your couch, then that would be the most ideal location for this project.

Flip the wooden magazine rack or folder divider so that the sides are facing upward. Fit its bottom and side to the corners of your living room wall.

Make sure that the placement is level with your couch. This will make it easier to reach when you need to get something. Measure the distance well.

Once measured, secure the magazine rack by drilling screws into it through the wall.

You may also opt to apply wood stain or paint before attaching the shelf to the wall.

You can now place decorative pieces on them.

The Wall of Books

If you have a lot of books, a wall shelf is one of the best things you can create in your living room. It doesn't have to be a plain bookcase, of course, because you can put all kinds of things. Instead of paintings and other decorative pieces, wall shelving gives character the room and decorates it in a very interesting way.

Supplies:
Wooden planks
Wood glue
Hammer and nails
Sand paper
Paint and brush

Instructions:

Measure the dimensions of the wall that you wish to work with

Cut the wooden planks in two different lengths. The longer ones will form columns and the shorter ones will form the rows

Arrange the different pieces, to build the wall shelf

Run sandpaper through the wood, to make sure that every surface is smooth

Paint the wood in a color that will suit your room. White is a safe color because most walls are white, making the whole thing blend well

Arrange your books, frames and vases on the shelf. Arrange everything neatly so that they look good

Vintage Trunk Coffee Table

Do you have a vintage trunk lying around unused? Maybe it's a hand-me-down from your parents or grandparents, and you do not really know what to do with it. Well, you can turn it into a coffee table, and give your living room some rustic appeal.

Supplies:
Vintage luggage
Stencil
Paint
Table legs (4)
Sand paper

Instructions:
To elevate the rustic appeal of your existing vintage luggage, run sand paper along the entire surface of the luggage
Attach the table legs to one side of the trunk, so that you form a table with the trunk lying on its side
Get a stencil and attach it to the "top" side of the trunk. Choose a design that will match the look of your room
Paint the luggage. Before doing so, you may want to add other things, such as screws and locks—or you may keep it as it is

If you love to travel, this vintage luggage is going to give you that feel. It's got character that you cannot get from anything else. So, it's uniquely beautiful.

Baskets Under Coffee Tables

Coffee tables look nice in the living room, but the space under the table is often wasted. This design turns the space into storage, so that you can maximize everything space you have. If your coffee tables are not designed with a lower layer, such as the one in the picture, you can add that bit so that you can put boxes on it.

Supplies:
Coffee table
Wood plank optional)
Decorative baskets

Instructions:
If your coffee table does not have a lower level, you can add one to it, by simply bolting a wooden plank in place
As for the baskets, you have the choice to get store-bought baskets but you can also make your own, and give each one of them your personal touch

Decide what you want to put inside each box. You can put albums, magazines, books, and so forth
Arrange each basket neatly, under the table

It's simple and straightforward—it definitely does the job of maximizing all the space you have under the coffee table.

Under the Couch Storage

You have storage under the coffee table—and you can also create storage under the couch. The design theory simple: if your couch presents with some elevation and there is space between the couch and the floor, you can use it for storage. In this design, you are creating a "drawer" to perfectly fit the space.

Supplies:
Carpenter ruler
Wood
Wood saw
Drawer handle (1)
Wood varnish
Wood glue
Sand paper

Instructions:
Measure the dimensions of the space under your couch
Cut the wood according to your measurements. You should have one large rectangular sheet big enough as the couch, two large rectangular planks to form the length of the drawers and four smaller rectangular planks forming the sides and partitions of the drawer so that you have 3 containers
Run sandpaper through the wood to make the surface smooth
Attach your chosen drawer
Apply wood varnish and let it dry
Arrange the things you wish to store under the couch. You may store books and magazines, albums, pillows, scarves and so forth

The space under the couch will only accumulate dust if you do not utilize it. This design is fairly straightforward, but it absolutely useful.

Cabinet-on-the-Go

Just before you get out of the house, you need your essentials. You'll need your car keys if you're going to be driving; and you'll need to have easy access to a few other things—the umbrella because it's pouring outside, your sunglasses, because it's sunny, the dog leash, and so forth. This cabinet is important by the door, because as soon as you enter, you can put your necessities in there—and before you head out, you know it's just there where you'd left them.

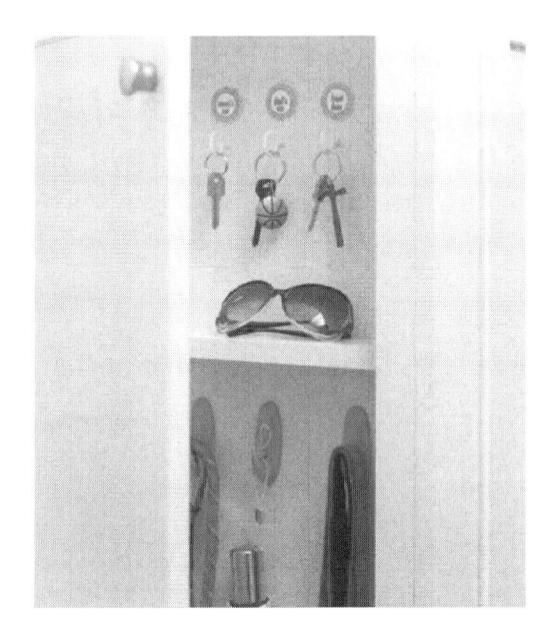

Supplies:
Wooden planks
Cabinet handle/knob
Wood saw
Wood glue
Hammer and nails
Sand paper
Nails
Plastic hooks
Double-sided tape

Instructions:

Determine the size of the cabinet your wish to build. It will depend on the space you have and the number of things you wish to put inside, but it shouldn't be so big.

Depending on the size, you will need 2 large rectangular sheets to serve as the front and back of the cabinet, 2 long rectangular pieces to serve as she sides, and 3 shorter rectangular pieces to form the top, bottom—one of the pieces will serve as a partition to be placed inside the cabinet.

Put all the pieces together, using wood glue, but you may also reinforce them with nails.

Sand the surface to make it smooth, and paint it in the color of your choice. It's good to match it with the color of the walls so it can blend.

Bolt the cabinet to the wall and make sure it is secure.

Attach the hooks to the cabinet wall. Keys will go on the top row and other things will go at the bottom.

Attach the cabinet handle or knob,

Instead of simply attaching hooks on the wall, you can hide everything inside a cabinet and deal with the clutter, effectively.

Piano Shelf

Thinking of installing wall shelving that's versatile and definitely visually satisfying? This design is laborious but it is unique and absolutely amazing. Basically, you attach identical pieces of wood in a single row or two (even more) and you should allow it a hinge movement that permits 90-degree extension. This means that at 0-degrees the piece is upward and at 90-degrees it is perpendicular to the wall. Install enough "keys" throughout the length of the wall.

Supplies:
Wood
Wood saw
Paint and brush
Drill and screws
Metal rods

Instructions:
Determine how long you want your shelves to be. Prepare a long strip of wood that would hold the metal rod.
Prepare identical pieces of wood to form the keys. It is not perfectly rectangular in shape—one side is wider than the other—so that it cuts diagonally to the other end where it should be narrower.
Punch holes big enough to fit the metal rod on every piece of wood.

Sand and paint all the pieces, making sure it is smooth.
Bolt the long piece of wood (the frame) to the wall. Make sure it is secure.
String all the keys into the metal rod, and attach the rods to the frame. Check the hinge movement of each key.

It seems rather laborious but the finished product of you your piano shelf is going to look absolutely amazing. You can move the shelves around anytime—and you can keep changing things around—that's the beauty of this unique design.

The Boxing Ring Shelf

Have you seen a boxing ring? The box is lined with some sort of rubber string around so that players appear to bounce off them when they collide with it. This design gives slight concealment of the contents of a shelf using a thick rubber string. The shelf is straightforward, really, but instead of keeping it open, you let a rubber string run horizontally, to almost curtain and cover the shelf. This means that if you need something, you have to pull open to create a gap.

Supplies:
Wooden sheets
Wooden cylinder/rods
Wood saw
Wood glue
Hammer and nails
Sandpaper
Varnish and brush
Thick rubber string

Instructions:
Cut the pieces of wood accordingly. You need 3 rectangular sheets to form the bottom, back and top of the shelf; and you need two square sheets to form the right and left sides of the shelf. Take a wooden rod and cut it into small pieces. It will form the feet of your shelf.
Bring all the pieces together with wood glue; and secure these pieces with nails. Make sure that it is sturdy enough to carry its contents.
Sand the surface to make it smooth and paint wood varnish to elevate its look. You may choose to use paint instead of varnish, if your aesthetic demands it.
Drill small holes on the sides of the shelf you have just finished; and like a shoelace, string the rubber from the bottom to the top, following a horizontal line. Make sure that the string is taut and secure so that it doesn't sag. It will look better when the string is tight.

If you're going to install shelves—make sure they bring a unique character in the room so that it's more than just extra storage space. This piece is surely decorative and it's going to look lovely in your living room (or any other room in the house).

Crates Under the Bench

Do you have benches in your living room? If you have one and you think you're wasting the space under the bench, then here is a good idea that you can use to maximize that space.

Supplies:
Wooden crates
Wheels
Metal handles
Drill and screws
Wood varnish and brush (optional)

Instructions:
Determine how many crates you can fit under the bench
Obtain the benches and decide if you are going to finish it with varnish or keep it raw as it is
Add the metal handles to one side of the crate. This side will be the one that's exposed, so you can pull the crate out, when you need to take something.
Attach the wheels to the bottom of the crate. While the wheels are not exactly necessary for the design, it will surely make it easier for you to

pull out a crate when you need it, if there are wheels installed at the bottom.

Telly Under the Table

Here is a creative idea if you want to provide a television for the room, but do not wish to have it out when it is not in use.

Supplies:
Center table
Wood saw
Drill and screws
Hinge joint
TV bracket

Instructions:

Find a center table with a wide and deep enough "table top". If you cannot find one, you may construct one from scratch.

Cut the top to remove the roof of the table.

Reattach one side of the "roof" of the table with hinge joints throughout the entire length of the table. You may also add hinge joints on the right and left side, and these joints will lock the table top in place.

Attach a sufficient size flat screen television to the underside of the table top, using a wall bracket. Choose a television that's not too heavy, so that the wood can carry its weight. You may also consider changing the quality of the wood, so that it would be better able to carry the weight of the television.

Pull-out Desk Under the Table

Here is another centre table idea that's going to add significant storage to your living room.

Supplies:
Wood
Wood saw
Sandpaper
Paint and brush
Gliding mechanism
Drawer handle/knob
Hammer and nails

Instructions:
Prepare the wood. You will need a few pieces—a large rectangular one for the table top, two smaller rectangular ones for the sides of the table, one small rectangular piece to seal one end, and then you need to a few more pieces for the drawer. You'll need one large rectangular piece for the bottom, two smaller rectangular pieces for the sides, one small piece for the back side of the drawer and the large rectangular one to form the drawer door.
Assemble the center table, so that you will have one side open to accommodate the drawer. Make sure the structure is secure enough to stand on its own, and should function effectively.
Assemble the drawer, securely.
Run sandpaper through the surface to make it smooth and apply paint. To give the table a nice distressed look, you may run sandpaper on the painted surface, before polishing it.
Install the gliding mechanism, so you can give the drawer some ease to go and in out of the center table.
Attach the drawer handle/knob and fix it securely.

Pictures Behind Picture

If you want to have a television, but you do not want it to dominate the living room, you can apply this clever design. Perhaps you have some pictures or paintings that are large enough to hide the full size of your television. If you do, you can convenient hide one among your collection of pictures and paintings, without anyone ever knowing that there is one concealed.

Supplies:
Framed picture or photograph
Wood saw
Sandpaper
Wall bracket
Hinge bracket
Drill and screws

Instructions:
Find a set of frames that's large enough to conceal a television. Approximate the size of the indentation you need to make to fit the television. Create this space, as needed. Obviously, a wood surface will be easier to tackle than a cement of concrete one. Nevertheless, you shouldn't have much trouble creating this indentation.
Attach the wall bracket and bolt the television to the wall. Make sure that it is securely placed.
Attach the hinges to one side the framed picture or photograph, and make sure that it opens and closes with much ease.

Chapter 8 - DIY Projects for Decluttering your Kitchen

The kitchen is a potential messy place because of the appliances, tools and equipment that complete it. If the kitchen is fully functional, and you are an avid cook, your kitchen will be fully-stocked and there will be a lot of potential mess to deal with.

The big dilemma is deciding on priorities—do you use the blender more than the steamer? Positioning your appliances, equipment and tools will affect the level of functionality you achieve. So, you have to organize everything so that it improves your work flow.

If you are big on cooking and your kitchen is housing lots of things, here are amazing decluttering tips that you can use to keep things nice and neat:

Pots and Pans Holder

Pot and pans are very bulky. But this design is going to free up a lot space. It involves hanging the lids on the cabinet door, so that you can stack the pots and pans on top of each other. This saves a lot of space and allows you to maximize what little you have.

Supplies:
Plastic hooks
Double-sided tape

Instructions:
Measure the size of the lids of your pots and pans
Precisely position 4 plastic hooks so that together, it can securely carry a single lid/cove.

Use quality double-sided tape and hooks. You do not want your lids to fall and break on you, right?

Grocery Bag Holder

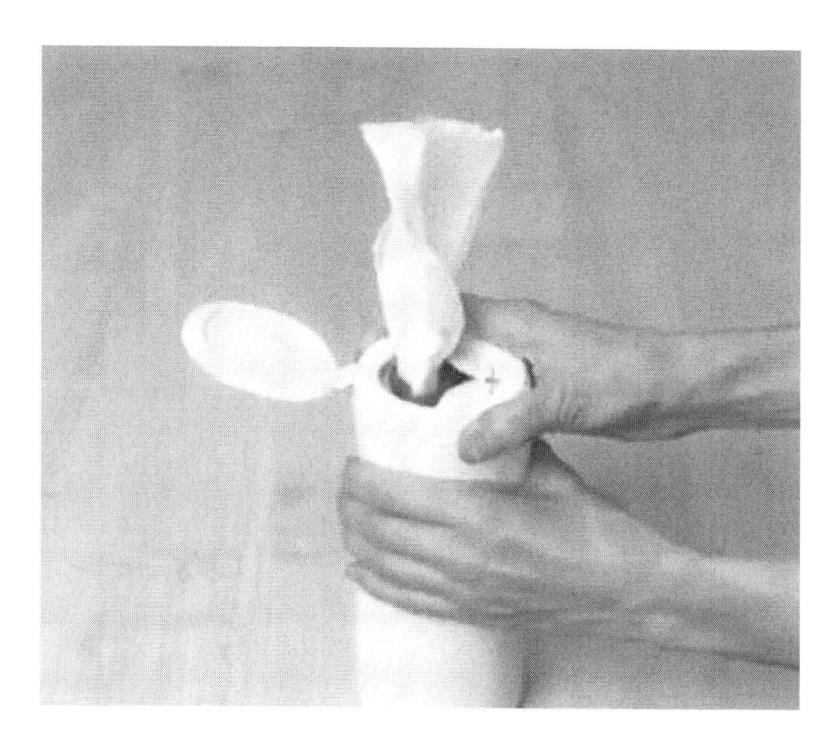

Supplies:
Empty Tissue Box or container

Instructions:
Inside the door of your kitchen cabinet, attach an empty tissue box. Use this to store empty grocery bags for you to use as trash liners or packaging.

Tension Rod Cleaners

Utilizing the space under the sink is always a good idea. But since the pipes make it difficult for you to store things that are bulky, here's an idea making use of tension rods, so you can conveniently hang spray bottles of various cleaning agents, and other stuff.

Supplies:
Tension rod

Instructions:
Hang a tension rod in the cabinet underneath the sink
Hang the spray bottles as well as things such as rugs and cleaning gloves

By letting the bottles hang, you saved a lot of space and this means that you can put more things inside, by exercising your creativity.

Lazy Susan for Pots and Pans

Supplies:
Stud finder
Pencil
Tape measure
Paper
Power drill
1/8-inch drill bit
Level
Wood shims
1 box of 3-inch grabber screws

Instructions:
Inside the cabinet wall, slide the stud finder against the wall until the device beeps. Mark the wall with a pencil at the centre of each stud where the stud is.
Measure and mark the distance from the corner of the wall to the centre of each stud.
Measure and mark the location of each stud on the back of the corner cabinet. Use the measurement you took before so that the grabber screw can fasten to the centre of the stud.
Using a power drill, drill 1/8-inch holes through the cabinet back at the marks made in the previous step.
Position the cabinet. Make sure the cabinet is level and only add the shims where needed, between the cabinet and the floor.
Secure the cabinet to the wall with the use of grabber screws and a power drill. Make sure the cabinet is level after fastening this to the wall.

Magnetic Knife Holder

Supplies:
Magnetic strip
Mounting adhesive

Instructions:
Select an area to hang your magnetic strip. Popular choices are over the sink, above the stove, or on areas where you do the most of your prep work.
Get a magnetic strip that is long enough to hold all your knives. If one doesn't fit, add another to split your knives into 2 separate rows.
Attach mounting adhesives at the back of the magnet.
Adhere the magnetic strip to the wall. You may choose to mount this any way you like.

Hang your knives with the blades pointing up. Organize them by size so you can locate the ones you need.

Cabinet/Pantry Dividers

Supplies:
Tension Rods

Instructions:
Install a tension rod inside your kitchen cupboard. Place similar items together or use it as a divider for various chopping boards.

Hanging Pot Holders

Supplies:
5' section of ½" conduit pipe
61" vinyl gutter
Mitre box with saw
61" long 1"x2"x6" board
73" long 8"x1"x6" board
Wood putty
8pcs 1/3" S-hooks
8pcs 1" metal O-rings
26pcs 5/8" wood or craft screws
6pcs 1 ½" wood screws
Sandpaper
Paintbrush
4 finishing nails
Stain and varnish or polyurethane
Wood glue

Tape measure
Permanent marker
Drill with small drill bit
Large D-rings for hanging
Wall-mount anchors

Instructions:
Cut vinyl gutter and 1x2x6 board to 61 inches.
Cut out 8x1x6 board into three sections: one at 63 inches long and the other two at 5 inches long. Stain wood boards as desired.
Find the gutter's centre using a tape measure. Make a permanent mark every five inches in both directions from the centre.
Drill holes at all the marked spots. Make sure the holes are big enough to create a pilot hole for the small wood or craft screws. This will help avoid cracking the gutter.
Centre then attach the gutter to the 8x1x6 board using wood or craft screws.
Attach the 5-inch boards at the shelf's sides. Make sure they are snug against the back board and ends of the gutter.
Place a screw at the top, middle, and bottom of the face board then fill in the holes with stainable wood putty.
Screw the closet-bar brackets to the inside of each side-board.
Place S-hooks on rings and slide these rings into the conduit pipe.
Install conduit pipe in the brackets.
Using D-rings, hang finished shelf on a kitchen wall.
Hang pots and pans on your assembled hanging shelf.

Paper Towel Holder

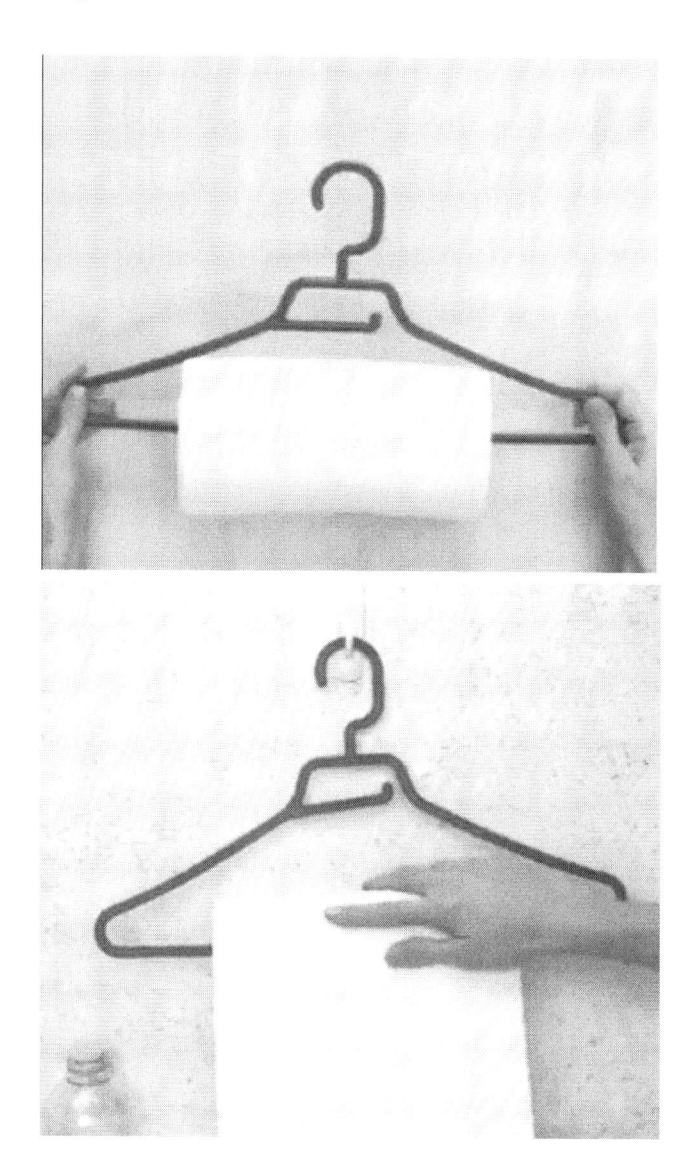

Supplies:
Hanger
Cutter or Pliers

Instructions:
Using pliers or cutter, make a cut at the centre of your hanger.
Take the roll of paper towel and pass it through the opening you made in the hanger.
Hang the hanger on a hook in the wall and use it to dispense paper towels at your convenience.

Egg Crate Organizer

Supplies:
Egg crate container
Scissors

Instructions:
Cut off the lid or cover of an egg crate. You may use paper crate or plastic ones as long as it can fit inside the shelf of your refrigerator door.
Place the cut-off egg crate and arrange it inside the refrigerator shelf.
You can use this to hold ketchup bottles, drink bottles, and any other items that need support.

Magazine Rack Organizer

Supplies:
Magazine rack

Instructions:
Take out all the cluttered kitchenware.
Organize these items into different categories and place them in separate magazine racks.
Put back in your cupboard and save space by this vertical shelving method.

The Vegetable Files

Vegetables are bulky and if you store a number of them in the kitchen, it can take quite lot of space. Here's a creative way to organize your vegetables in a kitchen shelf or cupboard. Choose a file holder or divider that's "meshed" so that your dry vegetables can breathe.

Supplies:
File Holder or Dividers
Labeler

Instructions:
Find file holders or dividers. It's best if they are made of metal and are meshed, so that it is not completely so enclosed, and the vegetables are still able to breathe.
Create labels for each container so that you can easily identify which veggie is in the file holder or divider.
Contain the veggies into their proper places.

If you are an avid cook, you will mean business in the kitchen. The vegetable files will absolutely be perfect for you.

Can Dispenser

Do you have a lot of canned goods that you do not know what to do with them? The thing with cans is that they are bulky so they take a lot of space. Storing them is going to be a challenge, so you can create this can dispenser so you can pack cans of the same kind in one dispenser, then stack them beside each other in the pantry.

Supplies:
Carton
Wrapping paper
Scissors
Tape

Instructions:
Gather your cans and group like cans together.
Measure the cans and prepare the cartons to the right height, width and length. Make the dispenser long enough so you can pack in a number of cans.
Assemble the cartons and build the dispenser using tape. Make sure to keep all the edges secure so that it can contain the cans effectively, but conveniently leave a slot open so that the box can dispense cans when you need one. Make the dispenser more aesthetically pleasing by covering the entire thing in wrapping paper.
Put similar cans into their assigned box and stack the boxes beside each other.

This design is going to make the pantry so organized and it will free-up a lot of space so that you can put more things inside.

Refrigerator Containers

The refrigerator is one of the most cluttered appliances in the kitchen. It holds all kinds of things and a lot of them get forgotten inside.

Supplies:
Tupperware
Labeler

Instructions:
Take out everything from your refrigerator and decide which ones you will save.
Assign each food product into its own Tupperware. Make sure to they are of the right size and label them accordingly.
Stack them properly. Arrange them in such a way so that you can see what you have inside, the moment you open the refrigerator door.

This will not only organize your refrigerator; it will make it look cleaner than it usually is. This will ultimately reduce spoilage, so less food gets wasted down into the bin.

Recipe Post-Its

Do you love to cook? Do you collect recipes? You can collect recipes from books, magazines, websites, and other places; and here is a great idea you can use to keep them all organized. Post-its do not take a lot of space. They come in different colors, so they're perfect for categorizing and they're convenient for use because of the adhesive feature.

Supplies:
Colored post-its
Recipes
Pen

Instruction:

Gather up the recipes you wish to collect. Categorize them into beef, pork, chicken, seafood, salads, pasta, soups, desserts and so forth. Assign a color to each category and start building your collection by copying the recipes onto the post-its.
Stick them together, by category or color, and start cooking.

You can keep the recipes on the refrigerator door or you can have it on the pantry door. It doesn't take so much space, so you can have them anywhere you want really.

Spice Frame

One of the most important things you can have in your kitchen, is a generous spice collection. The most enthusiastic will allocate space for his precious ingredients and this is a create way to do it because it saves space to have places to hang on the wall.

Supplies:
Large frame
Metal tray (magnetic)
Magnets
Metal spice cans/containers
Labeler

Instructions:
Take the glass out of the frame and place a metal tray on the slot.
Take them small spice cans and install magnets at the bottom of each can.
Label each can/container
Contain the different spices into their assigned containers then replace them into the metal tray. Make sure that the magnets are secure.
Hang the frame on the wall, near the stove so you can get to them conveniently, while cooking.

Keeping your spice collection this way is a very creative thing to do. It gives you easy access to your ingredients, so you can use it conveniently.

Hanging Cans

You need all kinds of containers for the things you keep in the kitchen and the best space-saving containers are those that are hung on the wall. It utilizes space that is otherwise not being used, and if you make these hanging cans, your clutter will look good hanging on the wall.

Supplies:
Curtain rod
Tin cans
Flowering plants
String/rope
Drill and screws
Paint and brush (optional)

Instructions:
Bolt the curtain rods to the wall.
Gather a few tin cans—about as much as your rods can carry. You may paint the tins to match the color of your kitchen, or you may keep them as raw as they are, depending on the aesthetic you are trying to achieve.
Punch holes on one side of the tin can and a string or rope, tie the cans in place along the length of the rod.
Decide on what you want to put into each can. Leave some cans unassigned and put dried or fresh flowers into these empty cans to elevate the aesthetics of the hanging cans.

You can put fresh flowers or artificial ones, for decorative purposes. You can also keep your fresh herbs in the extra cans.

The Spice Steps

This is an easy and inexpensive way to showcase and organize your spices in the kitchen. It's not so sophisticated, a design, but it is convenient.

Supplies:
Wooden blocks
Double-sided tape/Wood glue
Paint and brush (optional)

Instructions:

Prepare wooden blocks in identical lengths.

Arrange blocks to make it look like a staircase. Fasten them together using double-sided tape or wood glue. You may or may not choose to paint them so that it will blend well with your kitchen's aesthetics.

You may make the "spice steps" as high as you want, depending on how many spice bottles you have in the kitchen.

Cool Bottle Opener

Do you drink a lot of bottled beverages in the house? While it is not hard to use a traditional hand-held bottle opener, a wall-mounted one will make things more convenient and quicker.

Supplies:
Bottle opener
Sheet of wood
Magnet
Paint and brush
Glue
Drill and screw

Instructions:

Cut hole at the back of the wooden sheet to accommodate the magnet that you have but do not cut it through-and-through.

Glue the magnet securely at the back

Paint the front and add some personal design to it

Attach the bottle opener on the front

Bolt the whole design on the wall

You do not have to keep looking for the bottle opener when you need to open a bottle of soda or beer anymore. Your opener is on the wall and the bottle caps do not make a mess on the floor. The magnet at the bottom is going to conveniently catch the cap as it comes off.

Spice on the Roof

We've shown you different ways to organize your spices. How about if you keep them hanging? This makes decluttering creative and this design truly makes your spices, conveniently within reach, while you are cooking.

Supplies:

Empty jars that's large enough to fit your spices
Labeler
Metal strip
Magnet buttons
Super glue

Instructions:
Get the empty bottles and transfer your spices into them and label the bottles accordingly
Get the metal strip and glue on magnet buttons. Make sure to properly space the magnets so that the bottles will fit
Attach the bottles by the metal lids and make sure that they are secure enough

This design makes use of space (the ceiling of the inside of the cabinet or the bottom of the hanging cupboard) that's otherwise useless.

Cabinet Door Spice Rack

The back of the cabinet door is often left unused and it's such a waste of good space, really. So, if you can utilize it, that's going to be amazing.

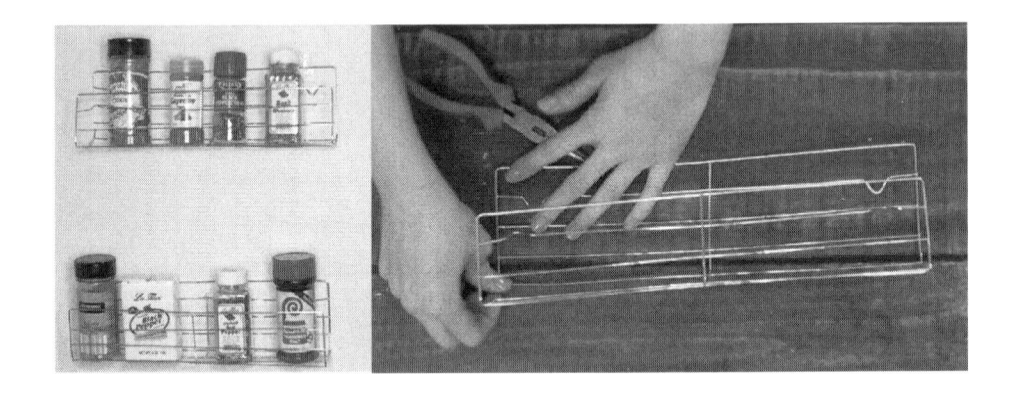

Supplies:
Metal tray
Pliers
Drill and screws

Instructions:
Find an unused metal tray lying around in the house and after making an approximation, fold the metal tray twice to create a rack out of it Bolt the rack onto the backside of the cabinet door. Make sure that it's secure enough to safely carry the bottles.

Best to install this rack on the door nearest to the stove so that you get easy access to it while cooking. It's inexpensive but it's pure genius.

Peg Board

A peg board is a creative way to stick things on the wall. The wall, as repeatedly mentioned, is often underutilized and a peg board allows you to have a fairly flexible organizational wall.

Supplies:
Peg wall
Drill and screws
Hooks

Instructions:
Bolt a peg board on any surface (door, wall, cabinet, etc.)
Scatter hooks all over the peg board
Hang loose items on the hooks, such as towels, spoons, forks, and so forth.

You can apply the peg board on the backside of a cabinet door, one side of the refrigerator, or the wall. The beauty with peg walls is that you can keep changing the orientation of things, so you can conveniently move things to best suit your need and function.

The Revolving Tray

Do you want an inexpensive way to store your bottles in the pantry? This revolving tray design is easy-to-make and it will make it easy for you to locate specific bottles.

Supplies:
2 plates
Set of marbles

Instructions:

Fill one shallow-bottom plate with marbles. A crystal plate is better so you can see the pretty marbles.

Lay the second plate on top of the marbles. Try to rotate the plate and check the ease of movement with the marbles.

Lay the bottles on the second plate and rotate it.

Who said you need an expensive mechanism to update your pantry? With two plates and marbles you have a magical revolving tray.

Plastic Bag Dispenser

You can always find good use for used plastic bags in the house, so keeping them is a good idea. You just need a good way to contain them, so you can get to them, in the easiest way, possible.

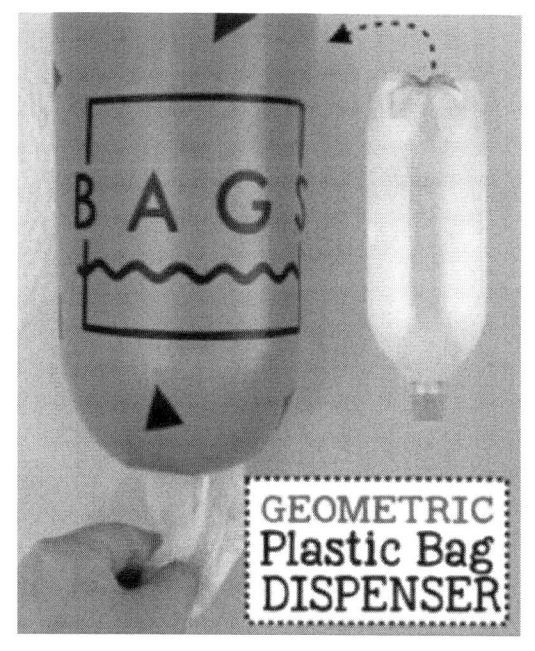

Supplies:

Large soda bottle
Paint
Sharpie pen
Scissors
Instructions:
Tip the bottle upside down and cut the bottom so that you have an open bottle
Decorate the bottle according to your aesthetic. You can even label it "plastic bags"
Arrange the plastic bags inside the bottle. Rolling them one after the other, is going to be the best
Take the lid off, and let one plastic come out through the spout
Hang the dispenser upside down

Just keep refilling the dispenser with used plastic, so it never runs out of supply.

Filing Your Cleaning Agents

Here's another creative use for your desk organizers. This makes brilliant use of the cabinet door and keeps everything neat and clean.

Supplies:

Desk organizer
Double-sided tape

Instructions:

Attach the desk organizer to the backside of the cabinet door. Make sure that it's secure enough.

Arrange your cleaning agents in the desk organizer

It's easy, but the simplicity of this design makes a lot of sense because it keeps things organized.

Hanging Fruit Basket

Here's a useful storage design for fruits (and other stuff, really). It makes good use of things you already have in the house, such a hanger.

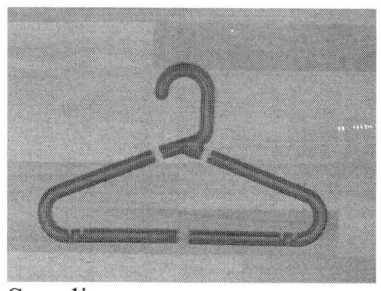

Supplies:
Hanger
Cutter
Plastic Tray
Glue
Instructions:

Cut the hanger in three areas. One in the middle of the bottom row; and then on either side of the hook, so that what you have are 2 v-shaped hooks.

Get a plastic tray, something deep enough to contain fruits, and glue the diagonal end of the "V" on both sides. Make sure the hooks are identically placed and check it for height placement; making sure that it will conveniently close, once you take it into the refrigerator.

Transfer all your fruits into the tray and put it in the refrigerator.

This design is also applicable for use in ordinary cabinets. You can do this in the pantry and you can contain other stuff, aside from fruits.

The Fruit Stand

Fruits are healthy and they're lovely to look at, so showcasing them in your kitchen in a creative way is going to elevate the look of your kitchen in an unexpected, but effective manner.

Supplies:

3 different sizes of pie trays
Metal cylinder
Small plants
Metal cutter/drill

Instructions:
Find 3 sizes of pie trays
Cut a hole in the middle of each tray and make sure they are properly in line. This hole should be big enough to fit the metal cylinder rod. Fix the rod through the three pie trays, and create three levels. Arrange the fruits in the fruit stand and add small plant plots, to elevate the aesthetic appeal of this design.

Don't the fruits look good this way? They will make a great centerpiece for the table and it make the fruits highly accessible, if you need a munch or two.

Pull-Out Pantry

The space between the wall and the refrigerator seems pretty useless, until you install a pull-out cabinet. It's an innovative kind of pantry, that's so creative and space-saving, you can put all kinds of things in it.

Supplies:
Peg board
Wooden planks
Wood rods
Drawer handle
Drill and screws
Wood Glue
Paint and brush
Sand paper
Drawer gliders

Instructions:
Measure the space in between the wall and the refrigerator, so that you know how much available space you have to work with
The peg board will form the back of your drawer
Prepare two long rectangular planks for the height of the drawers.
Prepare a few shorter rectangular planks for the length of the drawers—and afford enough pieces to give you enough partitions.

Cut enough wooden rods at the same length as your shorter planks. The rods will serve as stopper for the contents of your pull-out pantry. Assemble the drawer using wood glue. Bolt the shelves securely, and make sure they can hold what you plan to put in them

Sand the wood to make sure it is smooth, then paint the drawer and let it dry

Attach the wheel at the bottom

Secure the drawer gliders and position the drawer in its place

Attach the drawer handle and practice pulling the drawer in and out

Arrange everything in your new pantry

As you can see, the design comes with a "wheel" so that the entire drawer is easy to pull out. Take note that it does not have to be the space between the wall and the refrigerator. You can apply this design on any space, and you can use this design on any room—not just the kitchen.

Pyramid of Cans

Here's another good idea you can use to be able to store your cans without it taking so much space. Cans are bulky and they come in different sizes, so stacking them together can be very tricky but this simple idea lets you maximize all the space you have.

Supplies:
Metal trays

Instructions:
Get metal trays or any kind of tray that can fit standard size canned goods. Provide enough trays so you can use an entire shelf in your pantry for all your canned food
Arrange the cans in a pyramid. Put them on top of each other and try to have a system of grouping them, so you can easily find a certain can when you need it

This design is simple and it will hardly cost you anything. If you have the trays lying around the house, you do not have to spend anything at all.

The Potted Garden

If you cook a lot in your kitchen, you understand what value fresh herbs bring to the dishes you prepare. This kitchen idea is very simple. You will build an herb garden with mason jars, so you can freshly pick your ingredients when you need them.

Supplies:
Mason jars
Seeds to your choice herbs
Growstone
Soil
Labeler

Instructions:
Decide what herbs you want to plant in your potted garden.
Gather mason jars and label each jar accordingly. The jars on the photo were labelled using a chalk paint background, so that a chalk

can be used to write on it. You can do the same, or you can label your jars any way you want

Get your jars and fill each one up with grow stones or planting stone up to the middle. Fill the remaining half with soil.

Plant the seeds per jar and water each one of them

Of course, growing your herbs will require some patience and discipline. It is definitely easier to just buy from the grocery, but once the herbs are ready for picking, you will appreciate the value of your effort. Also, just imagine how beautiful the jars will look like in your kitchen.

Hanging Fruit Baskets

Here's another storage idea that's both functional and decorative. Of course, this idea is not limited to storage of fruits, as you can use it for your vegetables and other items too.

Supplies:
Plastic hooks
Double-sided tape
Metal baskets

Instructions:
Attach the hooks to the wall. Provide one hook per basket and make sure they are spaced enough so there is space not only for each basket, but also for you to get items in and out of the basket, as well.
Hang the baskets on the hook. Make sure the hooks are strong enough to carry the weight.
Fill each basket with fruits, vegetables or whatever you want to put in it

Fill the baskets with different color fruits and vegetables and your kitchen will look absolutely beautiful with fresh produce lining its walls.

Double Work Station

Have you ever worked in a small kitchen, with very limited space? Cooking can be quite demanding, especially baking. You have all your ingredients, tools and equipment overwhelming each other on the work space, so it helps when you can maximize the area. This nifty design is fairly straightforward. You create a small elevated workspace so that you have two-levels to utilize.

Supplies:
Wooden plank
Wood saw
Wood glue

Instructions:
Cut the wood in three pieces. Two pieces will serve as the stand or the legs; and the larger piece will serve as the table top
Put the components together with wood glue. Make sure that it is secure enough to carry anything you wish to put on it. You may or may not bolt it to the counter. Bolting it will make it stronger but leaving it unattached makes it portable, so you can have it where it's most needed.
Arrange everything on your kitchen counter.

This design is simple, but it works. You do not have to force yourself to work on a cramped space because you can create extra space just by creating an elevated table/tray.

Knife Organizer

The typical knife drawer is messy, cluttered and dangerous. If you make a mistake of grabbing a knife without looking, you can easily hurt yourself, so here is a simple idea that keeps the knives organized in the drawer. It looks neat and it makes grabbing a knife, as simple as it looks.

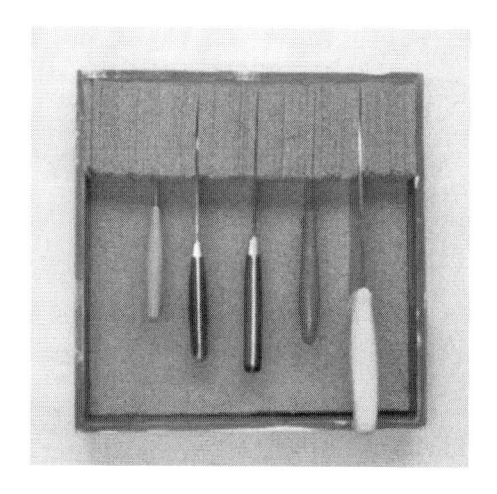

Supplies:
Corkboard
Scissors/cutter
Thing wooden sheets
Wood glue

Instructions:

Cut the wooden sheets to form a small tray of the same size as the drawer. Measure the dimensions carefully.

Form the square tray using wood glue. Make sure that the components are secure enough so that it doesn't break apart.

Line the entire surface of the tray with cork. Cut a square the same size as the tray to line the bottom of the tray; and cut small rectangular pieces of cork and line them on the top most part of the tray.

Make sure the layer of small rectangular corkboard is tight. One by one, insert your knives into the slits formed by each board. Lay this tray inside the drawer.

This design keeps your sharps in perfect order. The cushion makes everything safe and it will not cost you so much money to carry this out.

Peg Board Drawer Organizer

Everyone knows how hard it is to keep things organized in a drawer, especially when the things you're putting inside are of random shapes and sizes. Here is another cool application of the peg board that will help you keep your drawer in perfect order.

Supplies:
Peg board
Wooden rod or cylinder (2 sizes)
Wood glue
Sand paper

Instructions:
Attach the pegboard to the bottom of the drawer but leave a small space under—between the board and the drawer.
Create your pegs. Cut the smaller wooden rod so it's long enough to be pushed through the holes of the board. Cut the larger rod, tall enough to hold various things in place. Attach the small and large wooden rods together to create the "pegs".
Position the pegs according to what you want to put into the drawer. Arrange the things inside the drawer—use the pegs as a convenient partition or holder.

The beauty of this design is that it's versatile. You can move the pegs around the board, to accommodate anything you wish to keep in the drawer. You can keep changing the orientation of the pegs as often as the contents change.

Diagonal Organizer

The function of a drawer is limited to its size, and perhaps there are times when you position certain items diagonally, because they'll fit better in this orientation. Creating diagonal partitions for your drawer is a smart way to maximize the space in your drawer, so that you can put more things.

Supplies:
Wooden sheets
Wood saw
Wood glue
Sandpaper
Paint and brush

Instructions:
Measure the dimensions of the drawer
Cut the wooden sheets so that you form diagonal partitions that will create columns which will allow you to place various kitchen tools in the most efficient way possible
Assemble the pieces of wood and glue them on the drawer
Run sandpaper on the wood and pain it
Arrange everything in the drawer and appreciate the convenience this design offers

Orientation has a brilliant way of changing things. And by simply keeping the things in a diagonal position, you maximize the space—well enough to contain everything you need to put away.

Hidden Trashcan

The trash is never a good sight to see, no matter how nice your trashcan is. Thinking of a cool way to "hide" the trashcan is always a good idea. This one is simple. It makes use of the space behind the cabinet door, under the sink, so that a relatively useless space may be given its best function.

Supplies:
Trash can
Plastic hook
Double-sided tape

Instructions:

Pick a trashcan that's of the right enough size, to fit under the sink
Attach a plastic hook on the backside of the cabinet door, using a double-sided tape; and make sure it is securely attached and strong enough to carry a trashcan.

Hook the trashcan in place. Make sure that you can properly shut the door even with the trashcan in place

Hanging Soap and Sponge Dish

Almost everyone has a problem with a wet sponge or soap bars and other grooming material lying around messily on the sink. So, what if you can create something that puts things in order?

Supplies:
Plastic bottle
Scissors
Lighter

Instructions:

Find a plastic bottle that's thick and sturdy enough, but soft enough to be molded and formed.

Cut the bottle. Cut one side of the upper half and leave about one-third of the other side. Cut whole big enough so that you can fit the "organizer" into the faucet.

To bend the bottle, soften it with heat without burning it, then gently fold it and hold it so that it hardens in this position.

What a nifty trick—and it won't even cost you a thing, as the bottle and scissors are just lying around in your house.

Hanging Bottles and Things

Hanging things and utilizing the wall is truly a space-saving trick anyone wishing to declutter effectively, should master. This design is fairly straightforward. It basically transforms bottles and can into storage for many of your bulky stuff in the kitchen such as ladles, wooden spoons, and so forth.

Supplies:
Wooden sheet
Drill and screws
Adjustable ring with bolt
Mason jars or cans

Instructions:

Decide on whether you want to use mason jars or used cans

If you're going to use jars, you will need adjustable rings with bolts, to hold the jars at the neck. If you're going to use cans, make sure it is clean. You may or may not retain the outer covering of the can.

Bolt the wooden sheet onto the wall. Make sure that it's secure.

Bolt the jars or can onto the thick wooden sheet. Make sure that it's secure enough to hold what it's supposed to carry.

Arrange everything into the jars or cans

This idea, of course, is not limited to the kitchen. You may apply this design to various rooms in the house, for different things you wish to keep organized.

Paper Towel Drawer

Do you have an unused drawer in the kitchen? Perhaps you have one of those fake drawers that shows a fake opening, but does not really open into a drawer. Well, you can open that up and convert it to a paper towel holder. You ended up using space that's not being utilized and it looks pretty organized this way.

Supplies:
Retractable rod
Cutter
Wooden saw
Sandpaper
Paint and brush (optional)

Instructions:
If you're using an unused drawer, you just have to take it out. If the inner parts are not painted, run sandpaper through it and you may paint it, so that it does not look unfinished and raw. If you are using a "fake drawer" you have to do more work because you need
Dig a small notch to fit the retractable rod that will hold the paper towels. You can leave it as is, of course, but if you can create a notch, it will make the design more retentive

This idea makes it easier for you to get a sheet of paper towel. And this design keeps it cleaner than if it is on top of the kitchen counter, where it can wet and dirty.

The Hanging Cabinet of Fruits and Whatnot

Underneath the kitchen cupboard is space that's quite useful. And if you have nothing put in there, here's a simple design that will give you more storage space in the kitchen.

Supplies:
Wooden crate
Wood saw
Wood Glue
Paint and brush (optional)
Drill and screw

Instructions:
Get a wooden crate.
Cut it in half and set one half aside. Take the other half and cut it further, leaving only the edge of the crate.
Glue the smaller end to the other half of the crate at 40-degree angle. Make sure that it's secure enough to hold its contents.
You may or may not paint the crate to match the cupboard it's attached to
Bolt the crate and make sure it is secure.

You can use this storage for fruits, vegetables or anything bulky that you have lying around the kitchen.

Box for Plastic Bags

So, you've used up an entire box of tissue paper—do you throw away the box? Well no, because you can do something with it. You know your collection of used plastic? Well, you can save these boxes, decorate it, and stuff all your plastic bags. It keeps them organized and saves you a lot of space.

Supplies:
Empty tissue box
Wrapping paper (optional)
Double-sided tape

Instructions:
Decide if you want to redecorate or redress your tissue box with wrapping paper that matches the aesthetics of your kitchen
Wrap the box with wrapping paper, using double-sided tapes, so no tape is seen from the outside
Stuff the box with your plastic bags

By applying this idea, you save yourself some work because the boxes are already formed. All you have to do is dress them nicely in wrapping paper, if they do not already come in a nice design.

The Wall of Measurements

Measuring cups and spoons are often strung together like a set of keys and this makes them harder to use. Separating them from their "chain" scatters everything, so that it's easier to misplace them. Here is a cool design idea that puts your measuring cups and spoons at the backside of the cupboard door. It takes "storage and organization" in a whole different level because this design is absolutely reliable.

Supplies:
Blackboard
Wooden strips
Hooks
Drill and screws
Chalk
Paint and brush (optional)

Instructions:

Measure the size of the cabinet door and obtain a blackboard of the same size.

Bolt the blackboard to the cabinet door, making sure that it is securely in place.

Cut the rectangular blocks of wood and you may or may not paint it. Then attach it to the board to form two rows.

On the wood, bolt the hooks. Make sure to assign one hook for every cup and spoon. Hang them in ascending order of quantity.

Above each hook, label it according to the right measurement.

On the top portion of the board, write down the conversations, so that you do not have to keep on checking it when you're working on a recipe.

This design idea is so creative and useful—you turn the backside of a cabinet into something more than what it really is.

The Not-So-Fake Drawers

The fake drawers in the kitchen cabinets are quite annoying really. They look like drawers and they even have handles sometimes, but when you pull on it, it doesn't open. Here's a design idea that makes use of these "useless" space in a very creative way. It takes care of the mess you have lying around by your sink—and hides it so no one can see.

Supplies:
Wood saw
Hammer
Drill and screws
Hinge and bracket
Plastic trays

Instructions:
Gain access to the fake drawers either by sawing it open, or by punching it out from the inside. The latter may be a little hard if the bottom cabinets to not open. If you cannot do it easily, you may need to make new "covers" for your design.
Attach a hinge and bracket on either side of the "drawer" and attach it back to the kitchen counter
Obtain a rectangular plastic tray that's narrow enough to fit into the gap through the hinge opening.
Screw the trays in place—making sure that it is secure enough to hold whatever you decide to put on it.

Sponges are messy and unsightly. But by applying this design you hide the ugliness aside, without putting them away. It's conveniently within reach while you're working on the dishes, but it doesn't create any clutter.

Garbage Bags Under the Sink

Here's a simple design that will help you contain your garbage bags, so that it's easier to pull one bag out when you need it, and they're well out of the way so that they do not waste space anywhere else. In this case, it is put under the sink, an area that's often under-utilized.

Mostly a place for cleaning agents and whatnot, the garbage bags fit here, very well.

Supplies:
Metal bracket
Rod
Drill and screws

Instructions:
Measure the size of your garbage bag rolls
Obtain rods that are longer than your garbage bag rolls
Bolt brackets to the wall of the cabinet under the sink. Make sure the two brackets are at the right distance—long enough to fit the rolls of garbage bag and shorter than the rods to that it can hang properly. Make sure that it is securely in place.
Wrap the roll of garbage bag around the rod and hang it in place

This is simple and cheap—it also makes a lot of sense. This will make it easier for you to grab one bag.

Bottomless Drawers

Dish drying trays are so unsightly and when they're cluttered with thing, they look so messy. They take up so much space, but it's something you cannot really do without because—how else are you going to dry your dishes? This idea is so unique, but the features make so much sense, that it should be a standard for all kitchens.

Supplies:
Wood saw
Draining trays
Drill and screws

Instructions:
If you don't already have a cupboard over the sink then you have lots of work to do but let's assume that you do, so you will use that. Clear it out of its contents and remove the shelves—sawing them carefully, without destroying the walls.
Replace the wood with the draining trays. If you have old table top drains, you can just cut it and use them for your cupboard. It is very important that you secure the drains in your cupboards. They should be able to carry the load you're going to subject to it. You do not want your precious dishes falling and crashing on the floor.

Why do you have to let your kitchen suffer with the ugly dish drain? You can hide all of that with this creative design.

Pigeon Hole Spice Rack

Pigeon holes are often seen in lobbies of hotels and guardhouses of exclusive establishments. The design allows convenient storage of things from different people—and they are labelled accordingly so you can find it easily when you need it. This design is given a creative twist by turning it into a spice rack. With the bottles positioned with their bottoms out, it gives a lovely and colorful display that's going to be interesting in your kitchen.

Supplies:
Wooden sheets/planks
Wood saw
Wood glue
Sandpaper
Paint and brush (optional)
Labeler

Instructions:
Determine how many bottles you need to store because it will determine the number of pigeon holes you are going to make.
Measuring one bottle, and determining the design, cut sheets of wood to form the outer frames.
Using wood glue, form the columns of the pigeon holes. These columns will follow the height of your frame.
Cut small notches along the height of each column. These notches should be deep enough so you can insert small wooden sheets that will form the rows of each pigeon hole. Slide each sheet, to complete the design, and secure each piece with good glue.
Run sandpaper along the surface of the wood to make it smooth.
Decide if you want to paint it or keep the wood in its raw form.
Arrange your spices into their respective holes and label each slot so that it's easier to locate what you need when you're working.

Of course, your work will be so much easier if you do not have to build the pigeon hole. But if you're handy with woodworking, then you can properly customize pigeon holes that will be large enough to contain your entire spice collection.

Pull-Out Shelves

This design is a little technical, but it will effectively maximize the space you have. Cabinets are often spacious enough, but it's hard to put things in the deep end because it's harder to reach. Sometimes things at the back get forgotten and they waste away, unseen and unnoticed. This design conveniently takes care of that issue. The pull-out shelves give you easy access to the contents of the drawer—even the ones at the very back.

Supplies:
Wooden trays
Glider mechanism
Drill and screws

Instructions:
Find wooden serving trays that will fit into your cabinets. If you cannot find them in the exact size, you may need to make your own trays.

Apply the gliding mechanism on the trays and the cabinet. Plan what you are going to put in the trays so you can adjust their placement to fit your requirement. Check that the trays glide in and out, with much ease.

Arrange everything in the trays.

This design doesn't seem so much but it will definitely improve the function of your cabinets.

Pull-out Doggy Drawer

Do you have a pet? Here's a cool idea that will get rid of the doggy bowl clutter on the floor. Are you always tripping on the doggy bowl and do you wish there's a better way to contain them so that do not take up so much space? This pull-out drawer idea is an amazing design—you pull it out when it's time for your fur baby to eat and you close it when he's done.

Supplies:
Wood
Gliding mechanism
Cabinet handle or knob
Wood saw
Wood glue
Metal doggy bowls
Sand paper
Paint and brush

Instructions:
Check the bottom of your kitchen drawers. Find a good space to punch a hole, so you can create this design. Determine the size your need. It will depend on the size and depth of doggy bowls that you will use. Punch the hole to begin installation. Make sure to clean the edges.
Build your drawer. You will need two large wooden sheets to form the top and bottom of your drawer, and three rectangular sheets to form the sides and back. Assemble the drawer by bringing all the pieces with wood glue—but leave the top behind. You may also secure everything together with nails.
Lay the two doggy bowls side by side on the remaining sheet—and trace their shape so you can cut out a hole to fit them in. Attach the top to the drawer.
Sand the wood to make sure it is smooth, and paint it. You may match the paint with the existing cabinet so that it blends.
Attach the gliding mechanism on the drawers and the existing cabinet. Make sure it glides smoothly.
Insert the doggy bowls into the holes you just made.

This design may involve some work but think about the convenience you create by applying this? You no longer have to deal with doggy bowl clutter. It's easy to take out, so you can clean them, and surely your lovely pet will have no problem with his new "dining area".

Hang Them Like Pipes

Here's another way for you to conveniently store your cooking utensils. Give them individual holders using pipe rings. If you do not want them bunched up in a single container, you can organize them this way (either on the wall or at the backside of your kitchen cupboard).

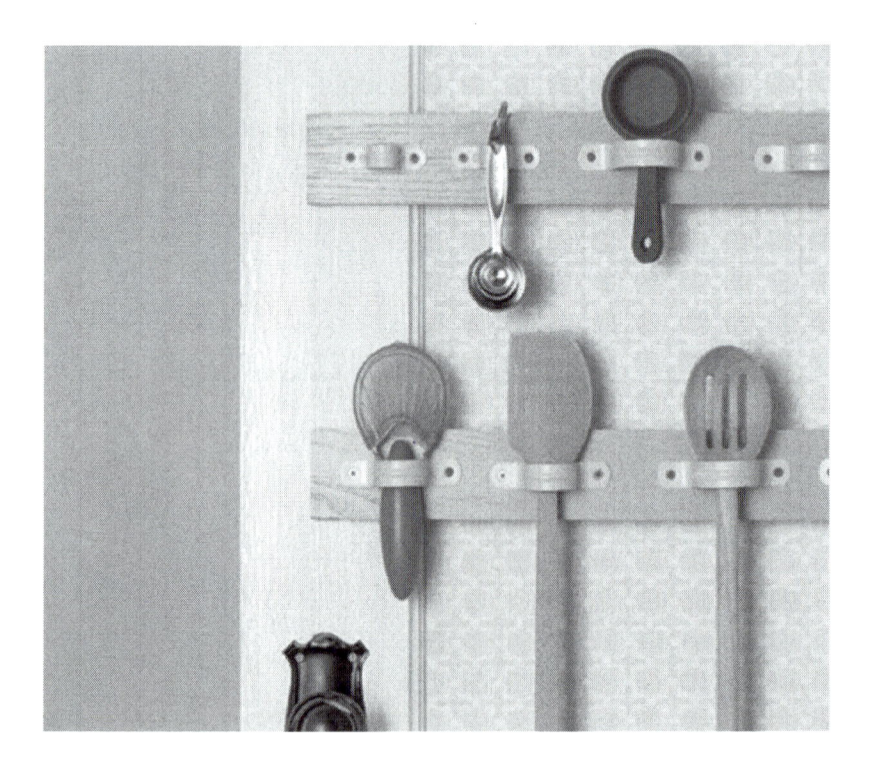

Supplies:
Rectangular piece of wood
Pipe wrings
Drill and screws
Sandpaper
Paint and brush

Instructions:
Determine how many cooking utensils or tools you want to display using your pipe ring design. This will determine the number of pipe rings you need, and the length of the wooden sheet you will use. Cut rectangular wooden sheets. You may organize more than one row, depending on the number of things you are going to hang and display. Sand the wood and paint it, then bolt it to the wall or the backside of your kitchen cupboard.
Gather your pipe rings. You may or may not paint it, to match the color of the board. Spacing each one of them properly, bolt the rings along the wooden sheet. Make sure each one of them is secure. Arrange your utensil and tools.

This design is best installed by the stove or the sink where most of the work in the kitchen is done. It is important that you think about these things when you're designing your room. You should always consider ease of function and movement within the room.

The Hidden Microwave in the Pantry

Whether or not you use your microwave often, it's always a good idea to clear your kitchen of all kinds of clutter. Most kitchen appliances can be put away. Coffee makers, rice cookers, and toasters are light and they can be tucked away in cabinets when they're not being used. Microwaves are heavy and they're not exactly portable—so finding a way to camouflage them in the kitchen is good. This idea is really simple. If you do not have an extra cabinet to fit the microwave, then you just have to make one.

Supplies:
Wooden sheets
Wood saw
Sandpaper

Hammer and nails
Wood varnish and brush

Instructions:

Let's say you have a free cabinet, and it magically fits your microwave perfectly. All you have to do is to lock in into its own row. Measure the width and length of the cabinet and prepare to pieces of wood. Attach to the wood to the cabinet and making sure it is secure enough to carry the weight of the microwave. If you need to put a bracket to reinforce the strength of your shelf, you can do so.
Sand the wood to make it smooth and run varnish over it, to give it a nice finish.

Tension Rod Dividers

Here's a good application of tension rods that's going to help clean you clean up the clutter inside your drawers. Keeping drawers organized can be a little tough if you do not apply some kind of system. Some people use containers to group things together and this is kind of the same with that, but instead of containers and trays, you can use this. It involves less work and it's very much flexible.

Supplies:
Tension rods

Instructions:
Determine how many tension rods you need to be able to separate the things you're going to organize; and figure out the design and partitions you're going to put
Fix the tension rods in the drawers and organize your things using them.

Backdoor Shelves

Here's a great way to utilize the backside of your cabinets and cupboards. The kitchen can be really cluttered, especially if you are fond of cooking. Here's a good pantry design that's easy to create.

Supplies:
Wooden sheets
Wood saw
Wood glue
Drill and screws
Sandpaper
Wood varnish and brush

Instructions:

Measure the space behind your cabinet or pantry door and determine how many extra shelves you can install, without blocking the existing shelves. You do not want to finish the work and realize in the end that you cannot close the door anymore, so planning this is going to be crucial.

Cut the sheets of wood. For every shelf, you will need 3 rectangular sheets that will form the front, bottom, and back of the shelf; and you will need 2 square sheets that will form the sides of every shelf.

Run sandpaper through the wooden sheets and apply varnish to it, to polish its esthetic.

Put all the pieces together, using wood glue, but leave the front side— so you can bolt the shelf to the door with much ease.

Attach the shelves to the backside of the cabinet with screws. Make sure that it is secure enough to hold what you're going to put in it.

Glue in the front part of the shelves and secure it in place. Make sure that everything is secure so that it doesn't break apart once you put the thing on them.

The Mirror Table

Most things have a single function, so when you are able to give something more than one, you elevate its purpose.

Supplies:
Mirror/Picture or Artwork
Wooden planks
Drill and screws
Sandpaper
Wood saw
Wood varnish and brush
Hinge and bracket
Lock or latch

Instructions:
Get a big enough mirror.
Frame the mirror with a strong enough wooden sheet that can function as a table. You will need a large piece of wood that will form the surface of the table. It should be bigger than the mirror you have chosen. You will also need two "U" shaped wooden sheets that will form the legs of the table. They should be the same width as the "frame", except that it is cut in half.
Sand the surface of the wood and apply varnish to it, so that it looks clean and smooth.
Using a hinge, attach both legs so that they form part of the frame when it is folded and they convert to legs, when they are opened. Afford some kind of latch that will lock the "legs" so they do not just fall off.
Bolt a latch or lock that will hold the frame in its place and will so keep it secure.

Cooking Files

The kitchen can contain a lot of large and bulky clutter such as trays and chopping boards. They come in random shapes so there seems to be no convenient way to stack them, so filing them in organizers that are ordinarily used for office files will keep things rather organized.

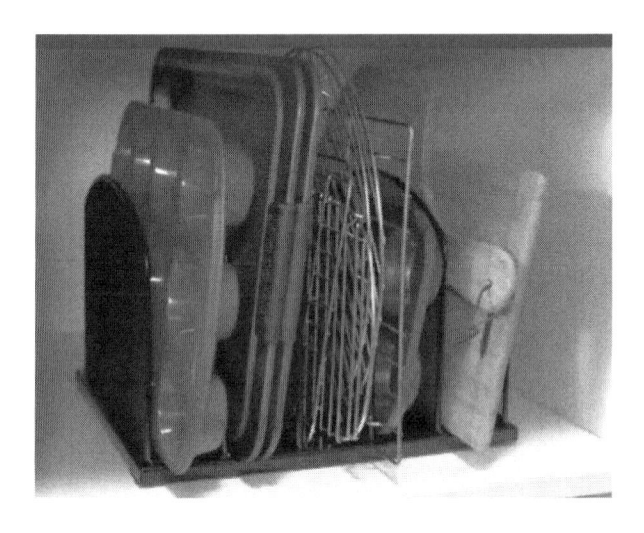

Supplies:
File organizer

Instructions:
Lay the file organizer in a big enough cabinet that would fit everything inside
Arrange the trays and chopping boards in each space

Cases in the Refrigerator

If you are tired of the mess and clutter in your refrigerator, then you ought to bring some system and order to it, even just through the use of cases or trays. You should be able to find properly sized ones that will perfectly fit the shelves. Achieve uniformity in size and appearance, because this will also provide aesthetic appeal.

Supplies:
Plastic trays and baskets

Instructions:
Obtain a number of plastic trays and baskets. Afford different sizes, so that you can conveniently store a variety of things.
Arrange the different items inside the refrigerator, into the different trays and baskets. Group them together in the most convenient way possible, so that you can get to them easily.

A clean refrigerator is one that is organized and pretty to look at. The baskets and trays will instantly improve the appearance of the refrigerator so that it will look absolutely spic-and-span. In this fashion, you shouldn't have trouble browsing through the contents of the fridge, so that you lessen the amount of spoilage.

Spice Drawer

Here is a good idea for your wee bottle of spices. Most people want their spice collection displayed in a rack, but some would rather give it a proper concealed space—somewhere unseen. A drawer, of course is a good concealed space. It should be space that's near to the stove, so that you can reach the bottles easily, when you need them.

Supplies:
Small bottles
Sharpie pen/Labeler
Small dish
Small measuring spoons

Instructions:
Obtain small bottles that are small enough to fit in a drawer, but large enough to contain your spices in a considerable amount.

Find yourself a spacious drawer that's big enough to contain the lot and the bulk of the bottles that you wish to contain. It ought to be near the stove.

Contain the different spices into the bottles and label each one for ease of identification. You may use your own handwriting or you may use a labeler.

Arrange all the bottles accordingly and then place a set of measuring spoons on a small dish, along with the bottles.

For the avid cook, this spice drawer should be the most significant drawer in the room.

Recipe Booklet

Where do you keep their recipes? Do you often trouble yourself going through books and online sites, every time you wish to whip something up in the kitchen? This idea allows you to collect different recipes, so you can organize them group them in different categories.

Supplies:
Clear book file
Clear book plastic sheets
Recipes

Instructions:

Gather all the recipes that you can manage either from different magazines, books, and websites. Make sure to collect enough of a variety so that you can build a nice collection.

Transfer all the recipes onto paper. You may have it typed up nicely, or you may keep them in your own handwriting.

Prepare labels that will help group and categorize your different recipes. You may categorize them in different ways: Breakfast, Lunch, Dinner, Desserts; or you may group them into type of dish: Chicken, Pork, Beef, Salads, Soups, Fish, Seafood and so forth.

Arrange all the recipes into the different categories and contain them in the nice clear book file.

Garbage bag holder

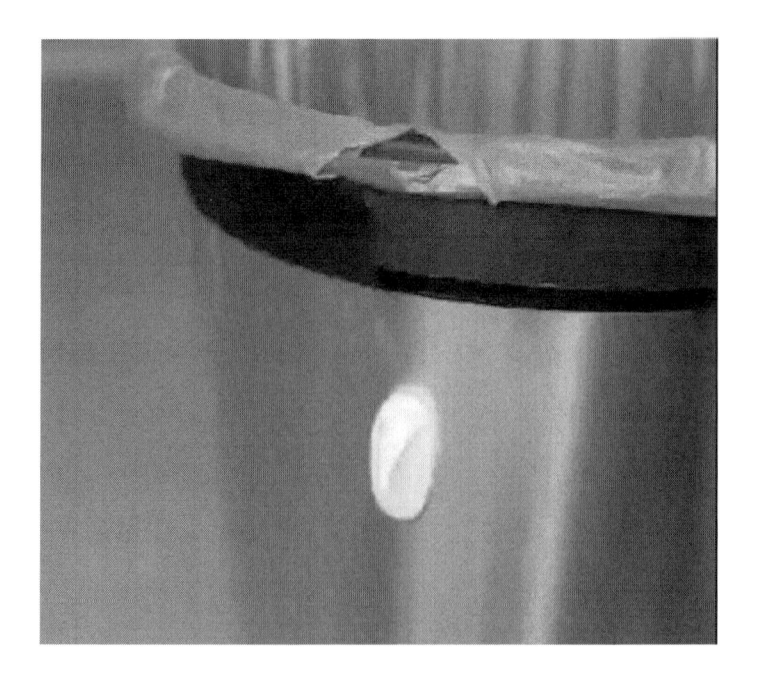

Supplies:
Stick-on hook

Instructions:
At the opposite sides of your trash bin, attach a stick-on hook on each. Stretch out the sides of your trash bag so that you can hook them to the stick-on. This method prevents your trash bag from buckling under the weight of the trash.
Secure and never have to deal with messy, cluttered trash bins again.

Chapter 9 - DIY Projects for De-cluttering your Garage

For the men of the house, this room is their personal sanctuary. This is where they spend a lot of their time either tinkering with the car or working on a latest do-it-yourself project. The storage room holds their most precious tools and equipment, and if this is not properly organized, you'll definitely have so much clutter to deal with and getting your hands on a shovel may be a "scavenger hunt" through the pile of mess in the garage.

Whether the garage is solely a storage area for your various amassed possessions, or it has been converted to a workshop, it is still a room that you need to keep in order.

Tool Shelf

Shovels, rakes, and other large tools are very essential tools for home improvement and cleaning, so if you are someone who has a lot of these tools lying around at home, then you need a tool shelf to conveniently contain all them in the garage.

Supplies:
Wooden planks
Wood saw
Nails
Hammer

Instructions:

Create a wooden rack/frame by cutting 10 long planks and 4 shorter planks.

Assemble the rack/frame using the long and short planks. The long planks will form the horizontal walls and the short planks will form the vertical walls.

Once the rack/frame is formed, bolt it securely to the wall.

Arrange all the tools into the bolted shelf.

You will never misplace your important tools anymore as you now have a perfect place to keep all of them in. Make it spacious enough so that it can accommodate everything.

Wall of Tools and Spools

Here's another idea you can use for the many lose things you have in the garage. This design gives everything a place to go; and by keeping your things organized, you make your life easier and more convenient.

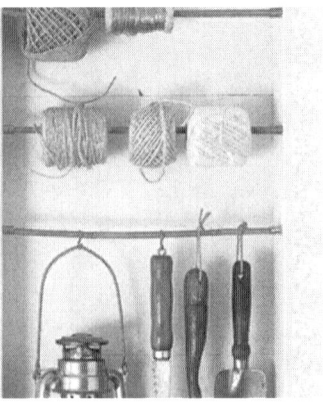

Supplies:
3 long wooden planks
Metal rods
Hooks
String/rope

Instructions:
Bolt the 3 long planks vertically, so that you form two columns.
Install the rods along the height of the two columns, giving yourself enough space for the different things you wish to hold.
Hang, tie and spool the different tools and things that you have. Do not cramp them together.

The wall of tools and spools is a creative way to keep your things organized in the garage. Instead of having a mess it will look as if you have your own craft store in the room.

Peg Wall of Tools

Peg wall are simple but very creative. It doesn't demand high level technical know-how but it does the job of keeping things organized in the most effective and convenient way possible.

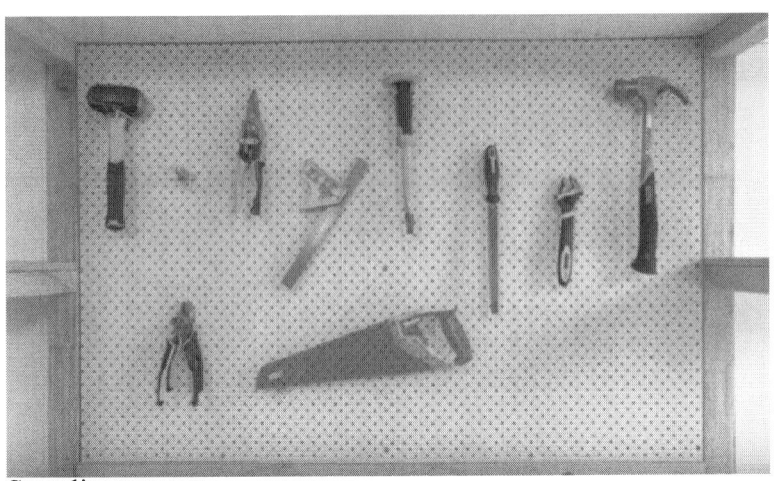

Supplies:
Peg board
Drill and screws
Hooks and nails
Tools

Instructions:
Bolt a peg board on the wall. You may incorporate it with your shelves or it could be a standalone wall.
Determine which tools you need to put on the peg wall. Using nails, keep them in place. Be strategic with your placement so that each one of them is secure.

Why keep your tools in a box that you have to rummage through every time you need something, when you can display them this way on your garage wall?

Hosing' Around the Tub

The water hose is bulky and often very hard to store because it can take a lot of space. This simple idea is cheap but it is effective—all you need is a tub.

Supplies:
Plastic tub
Drill and screws

Instructions:
Get an empty tub
Bolt it to the wall, from the bottom of the tub, and make sure it is secure enough to carry whatever you wish to put in it
Inside the tub, contain large items that you don't know where else to put
Outside the tub, wrap the entire length of the hose around it

This design keeps the hose, elevated, when not in use; so that it is kept clean. When you keep the hose lying around the ground it does not only get dirty, but there's a bigger chance for it to get punctured.

Utility Belt Tub

A utility belt, is wrapped around the waist, and worn as a belt so you can keep your tools near you while you're working. You can also wrap this belt around a pail when you're not using it. It converts a pail, of a single function, into something more.

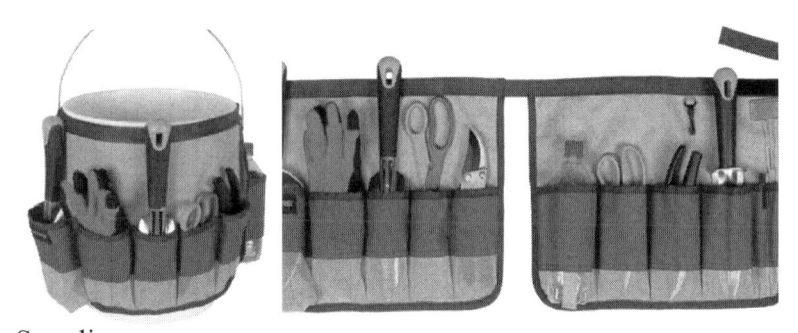

Supplies:
Utility Belt
Empty Pail

Instructions:
Arrange your favourite tools in a utility belt.
Secure this belt around the pail

If you do not want to wear the belt, you can just let the pail wear it. It's definitely an ingenious way to keep your most important tools in order. It still functions as a pail, but it can carry so much more than it usually does.

Screwed Bottles

A previous design featured hanging bottles using magnets. This design is different and it is much more secure because the bottle covers are screwed in place. This means that you have to screw the bottle from its cap to use it, but it's still fairly simple.

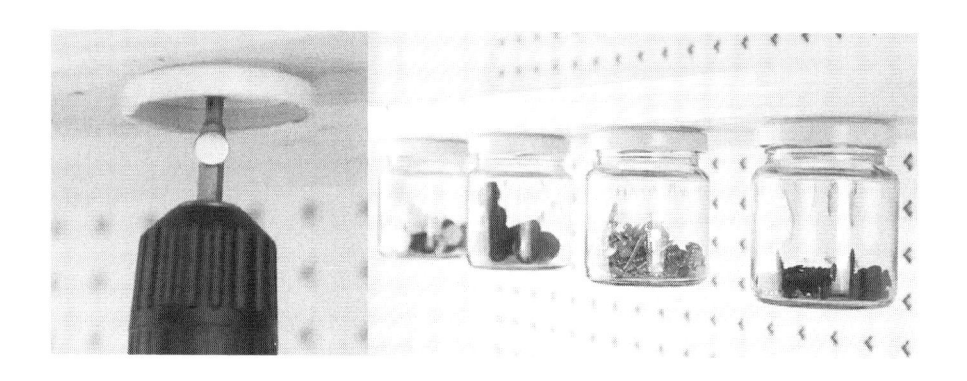

Supplies:
Small bottles with metal covers
Drill and screws
Screw driver
Labeler

Instructions:
Obtain small bottles and decide on what you want to put in them.

Approximate bottles into position. Drill holes for each bottle.
Remove the bottom and set them aside, while you screw in the bottle covers. Make sure the covers are secure; and use a big enough screw to keep them in place.
Create labels for each bottle so that it's easier for you to identify them. Replace the bottles to their respective covers

You may decide to put anything into the bottles. You can put screws, pins, nails, and so forth. Take note that this design is applicable for other things, and not just things in the garage. You can use this design for the kitchen and bedroom, as well.

Hanging Brushes and Things

Here's a cool idea that you can use for your brushes, knives and similar tools. For the brushes, hanging them will make it easier for you to dry them, after use. You can keep them dry and secure, when not in use, and gain easy access to them when you need them.

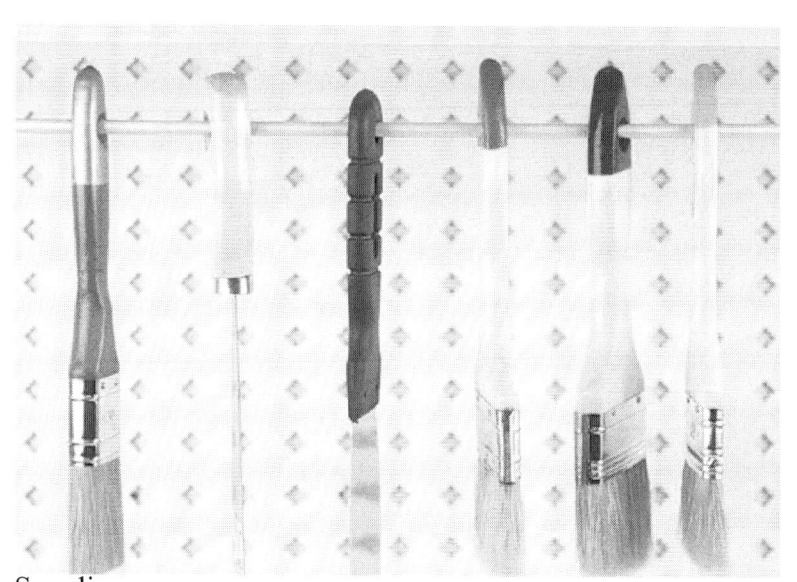

Supplies:
Metal Rod
Drill

Instructions:
Bolt a metal rod in place
Gather all your brushes and other tools, and drill of hole through their handles if they don't already have one
Thread the rod through the brushes and knives; and secure them in place.

We don't always get to think about everything but there is a perfect place for things, if you just allow yourself some creativity.

Magnetized Tools

Here's another good use for magnets. You can install this design on a peg board, or you can do this for any wall in your garage. Of course, it only works for metal tools, of course. You do not have to put stick magnets on the tools, as they are already made of metal, and have magnetic properties.

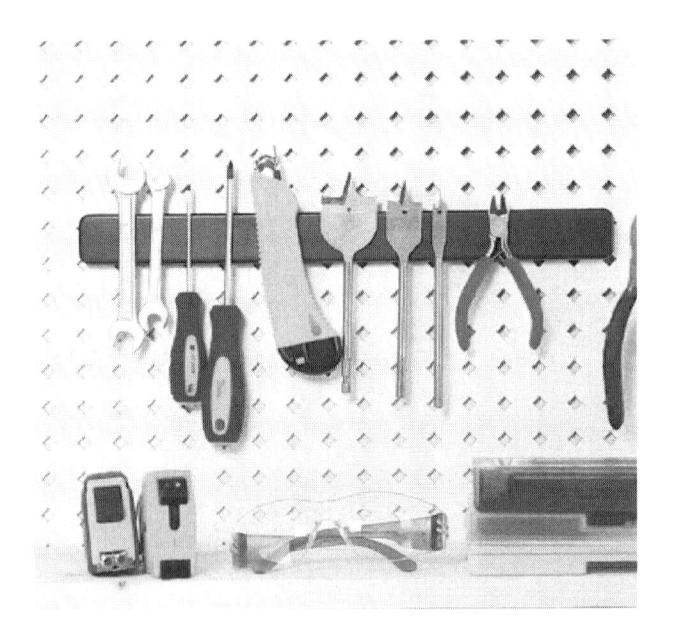

Supplies:
Magnetic strip
Drill and screw/double-sided tape

Instructions:
Bolt the magnetic strip on the wall. You may also bolt this on a peg wall, if that is what you have.

Arrange your metal tools along the length of the magnetic strip, making sure they are secure and easy to get to

This design may also be applied to the kitchen knives. They're metal and they can also be magnetized to the wall.

Cleaning Baskets

In most houses, the garage is also the storage room for various cleaning supplies; and here is a good way to organize your cleaning materials. It's fairly straightforward—it assigns a specific basket to a room, so that you have everything you need, in order to keep a room spic-and-span.

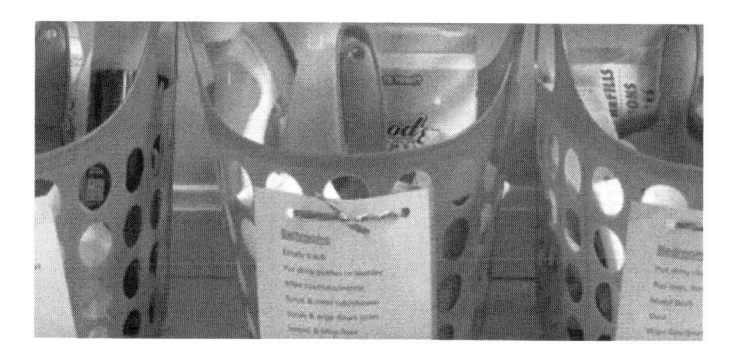

Supplies:
Plastic baskets
Collection of cleaning materials and tools

Instructions:
Determine how many baskets you need—by counting how many rooms you need to clean

Plan what type of cleaning materials and tools you will need, based on the type of cleaning you are going to do for a particular room
Contain the set of cleaning materials according to room, and make sure to stock them sufficiently.

This method of organization is simple but it keeps things in perfect order. You do not have to let these cleaning materials clutter your rooms because they're beautifully tucked in their own baskets.

Multiple Tape Dispenser

Tape dispensers are great for your stationery collection, but the trouble is that they are limited to one roll of tape. This solution allows you to organise multiple rolls of tape in the same place.

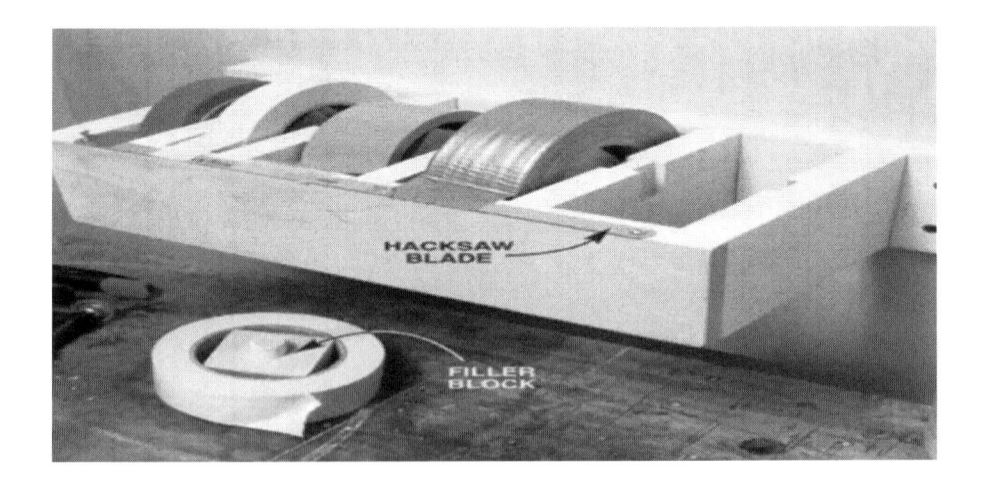

Supplies:
Rolls of tape
Wood
Wood saw
Wood glue
Sandpaper
Wooden cylinder/rod
Drill and screws
Hacksaw blade

Instructions:
Prepare the wood. You will need two large rectangular pieces to form the length of the tape dispenser. You will also need shorter rectangular pieces to form the sides of the dispenser, and the division in between tape rolls.
Create the filler blocks that will hold the tape. It should be big enough to lock into the core of the tape. Get a wooden cylinder/rod and cut small pieces then stick one each to the center of the block.
Take the smaller rectangular pieces and cut a notch on that will fit the filler blocks perfectly. Do a trial fitting of the blocks to make sure it fits perfectly and moves with ease.
Assemble the dispenser by putting together all the different parts. Make sure that you give enough space for each roll of tape, when you lay the dividers. Secure everything with wood glue and reinforce it when nails, if necessary.
Run sandpaper through the entire surface to make it smooth.
Bolt the dispenser to the wall. Make sure that it is secure.
Attach the filler blocks to the tape and install them into the notches.

Tupperware/Crates for Everything

If your garage is also your storage room, you might experience a lot of clutter. It is a good idea to find a good system to keep things organized— Tupperware or containers of different sizes will do the trick nicely. It will be even better if you used transparent ones with labels so that you can identify the contents easily.

Supplies:
Tupperware
Labeler
Shelves

Instructions:
Gather all your things and group them into categories, so that you can decide how many Tupperware and containers you will need, also what sizes will be best for the different contents.

As soon as you know what you're going to organize, you need to obtain the right containers and Tupperware. After which you have to prepare labels for each one, so you wouldn't be confused about where everything is supposed to go to.

Arrange everything in its proper place. Contain the small things where they're supposed to be, and then lay them on shelves.

You may use ready-made shelves or you may choose to build your own shelves for the garage, so that your containers will fit perfectly.

Hanging Ladder

The ladder can be very bulky, but if you're the type who does a lot of work in the house, then a ladder is going to be a necessity. Here's a practical idea so store the ladder neatly without taking too much space.

Supplies:
Wooden block
Wood saw
Drill and screw
Metal rod/post

Instructions:
Prepare 4-8 wooden blocks, depending on how large the ladder is. Make sure to cut it evenly; and make sure it is long enough so that there is good space between the ladder the ceiling.
Prepare the metal rods/post. There should be one post for every pair of wooden blocks. It should be long enough to fit the length of the ladder. Bolt the blocks to the ceiling. Make sure the pair of blocks are positioned properly, so that the rods may be fitted perfectly, and so that it can sufficiently hold the weight of the ladder's entire length. Attach the rod/post to the blocks, at either end. Make sure that it is secure enough.

Hanging Crates

Here's another option for the use of the ceiling. Often under-utilized, you can make good use of the ceiling and reclaim a lot of precious space. If your garage is also your storage, then it will be natural for you to have all kinds of clutter cramped into crates. Crating, is of course is good idea because it keeps things in order. Unfortunately, crates are large and bulky, so you have to be a little creative when you're trying to store them.

Supplies:
Wood
Sandpaper
Drill and screws
Hammer and nails

Instructions:

The design for the crate holders will depend on how big a surface, your ceiling can provide. One holder can hold 1-4 crates at the same time, depending on how strong you can reinforce the structure. Depending on the design you need, you need to build the crate holders, first thing. As soon as you have decided on a design, you can move forward to construction.

Prepare the wood. You will need a large sheet of thick wood that will form the base of the holder, two large rectangular blocks that will form the sides of the holder, and then two thin rectangular sheets of wood to form the notch that will hold the crates in place.

Assemble the crate holder with nails and screws. You have to understand that the crates are going to be heavy, depending on its contents, and the holders have to be very strong.

Bolt the crate holders to the ceiling. Make sure that they're properly secure, and can carry the weight of the crates.

This design is very creative, but it is technically tricky, so if you think you're better off finding an expert to work on this, you should seek help.

Pipe Holders

PVC pipes may be meant for plumbing, but why should limit yourself? Creativity and resourcefulness are about finding alternative uses for things. A used pipe may be ready for disposal, but if you make simple alterations you can turn them into creative holders for your large bulky tools such as shovels and rakes.

Supplies:
PVC pipes
Drill and screws
Labeler
Saw
Sandpaper

Instructions:
Find a good wood panel in the garage on which you can install the PVC pipe holder to, but if you cannot find one, then you will need to install a wood panel to the wall, first thing.
Gather your large tools to determine how many pipe holders you need to create.
Prepare your pipe holders. Choose a large PVC pipe that will fit even the larger tools in your garage. Cut them up into smaller pieces. One tool should be given about 2-3 pipes to hold them in place. Run sandpaper through the edges, to make it smooth.
Bolt the pipes to the wood panel. Make sure they are properly aligned with each other, so that you can easily position your tools.
Label the PVC pipes so that you can assign a specific slot for each tool and nothing gets mixed up.

Install this near the ground so that the tools are allowed to touch the floor, while being held in place by pipes.

Bike Pole

Do you have a bike? One bike might not be as challenging to store, but what if you are fortunate enough to own more than one? This design involves installing a pole that extends from ceiling to floor, with holders that will lock them in place.

Supplies:
Metal pole
Metal clamp
Drill and screws

Instructions:
Measure the height from the ceiling to the floor and find a pole that's long and sturdy enough to carry the weight of the bicycles.
Bolt the pole to the ceiling and the floor, making sure it is secure. Attach clamps along the length of the pole, this clamp should be securely bolted to the pole, and it should have a mechanism that will allow you to clamp onto the bike frame.
Hang the bikes by the clamps. Make sure everything is securely fastened.

Store the lighter bikes at the top and access them with a ladder when the time comes to use them.

Boot Crate

Do you have used crates lying around in the house? Now it's time to turn them into nifty boot crates for your outdoor boots.

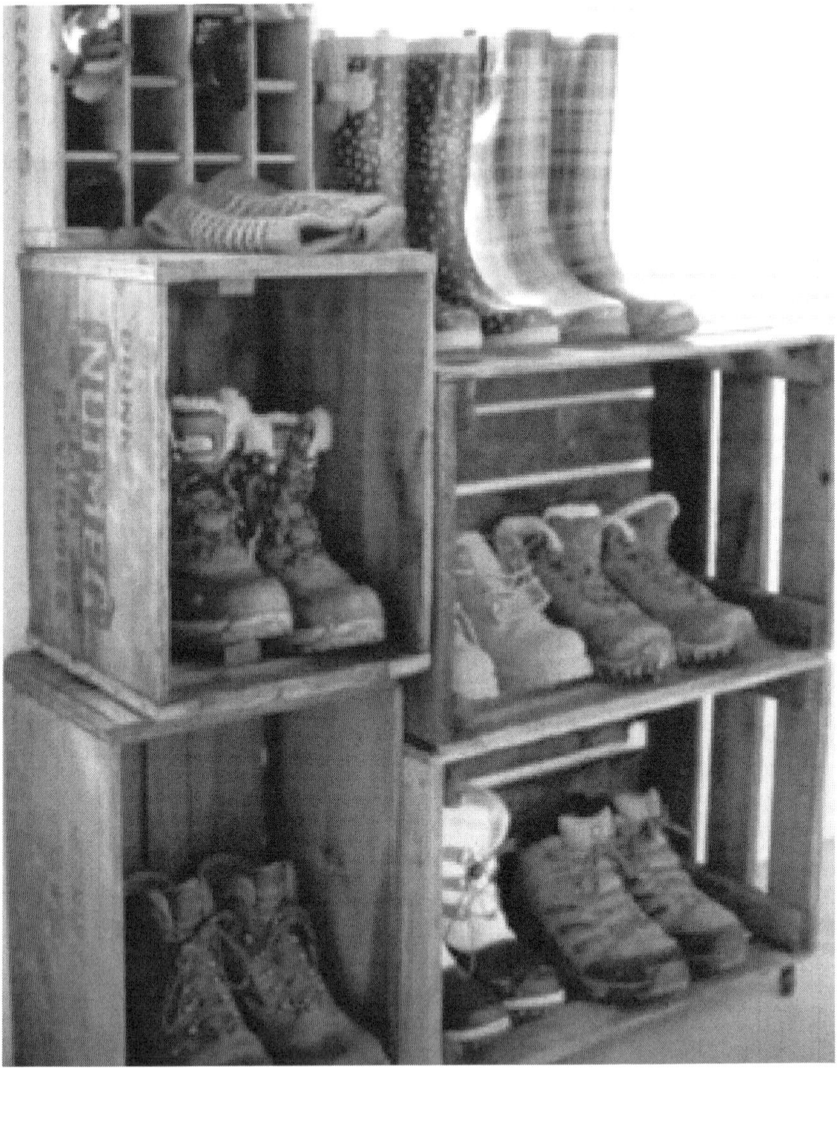

Supplies:
Crates
Hammer and nails (optional)

Instructions:
Gather all your boots to determine how many crates you need to have Stack the crates one, on top of the other. You may stack them simply, or you may choose to bolt them together with nails, so that they are quite secure. Some crate may be vertically oriented—some may assume a horizontal position.
Arrange your boots into the different crates.

You may also use the crates to store your flats and other shoes. But to maximize the space that the crate provides, you will need to create shelves within the crate, so you can put more shoes inside.

Recycling Cans

To play your part in saving Mother Nature, it is important to make an effort at recycling. One way is to dispose of recycled waste is to put them in their designated bins; another way is to reuse them for different functions. The latter reduces waste disposal and has the added bonus of saving cost.

Supplies:
Empty cans with plastic lid
Labeler
Cutter
Paint and brush

Instructions:
Gather metal cans with lids. Powdered milk or chocolate cans are good because they're dry goods and it will be easier for you to clean inside the cans very well.
Cut a small hole on the cover of the can. It should be big enough to fit what you plan to put through it.
Paint the cover the can. You can choose to paint it any colour, or you can choose white, as it looks nice and clean that way.
Label the cans accordingly. If you wish to assign more cans to more items specifically, you can simply label them.

Folding Work Table

Supplies:
Wood
Sandpaper
Wood saw
Hammer and nails
Hinge and bracket
Hook and screw

Instructions:
Determine the design you want for the table. This will depend on the kind of work you usually do. If your table tends to be quite busy, then you will need a big one; otherwise, a small table should be fine if you only do minimal work.
Prepare the wood. You will need a large rectangular sheet of wood to form the table top, and two wooden rectangular blocks to form the legs of the table.
Assemble the table and bring the pieces together. Attach the legs to the table top using a hinge mechanism, so that you can fold the legs when you are not using the table.
Attach the table top to the wall using a hinge mechanism so you can fold it.
Attach a hook system at the top of the wall, so it can hold the table up when it's not in use.
Run sandpaper throughout the entire surface of the table, and make sure it is smooth.

Why let a big table clutter the garage and storage? Easily reclaim extra space by applying this simple design.

Bicycle Hook

If you want to save floor space, you can hang things from the ceiling and keep them out of the way. The hook system is fairly straightforward; you attach two hooks to approximate the wheels and hang them up.

Supplies:
Hook
Drill and screw

Instructions:

Bolt the hook to the ceiling. Make sure that you space it well enough so that you can hook both tires with ease. Make sure it is secure enough to carry the weight of the bicycle.

Gently lift the bike to the hook and make sure it is secure.

If you have more than one bike, you can easily position the hooks beside each other. That way the bikes will be properly organized—in a single line.

The Sports Case

Do you keep a lot of sports equipment in the garage? Here is a nifty project you can use to create a dedicated space for them.

Supplies:
Wood panels
Wood saw
Wood varnish and brush
Sandpaper

Instruction:
Prepare the wooden panels. You will need a few pieces. You will need eleven pieces of rectangular panels, long enough contain the bulk of your equipment (when positioned horizontally), and long enough to hold the height of your long paddles and bats (when positioned vertically).
Assemble the case and secure the pieces. You need four panels placed horizontally, on the front and back of the case; and you will need one panel each to go on either side. You can also put one vertically-oriented panel in the middle, to act as a barrier between two sections. Secure the pieces together.
Run sandpaper through surface to make everything smooth and apply wood varnish to give it a nice polish.
Bolt the case to the wall.
Arrange your equipment.

Ball Case

Carrying on with the sports theme, another tricky thing to store are balls as they can be an eyesore if they are lying around all over the place. This project helps you to keep them stacked together in an organised fashion.

Supplies:
Ring metal
Thick metal wires/rods
Soldering iron and equipment
Thick elastic rope

Instructions:

Prepare the metal wires/rods and the metal ring. You will need two metal rings for the top and bottom, 3-4 large sticks/rods to form the back part of the case, and smaller pieces of metal sticks/rods to close the rings at the top and the bottom.

Solder the metal together to assemble the case. Make sure every part is secure.

Stretching it slightly, tie the elastic rope at the front of the case. This will serve as the "door" or opening of your ball case. You use elastic rope so you can stretch it and conveniently take the balls in and out of the case. Make sure the rope is tight enough so that it can hold the balls, but can still stretch.

Soldering iron is not very difficult, depending on the equipment you're using. If you think you cannot handle this work by yourself, feel free to find someone to do it for you.

Fishing Rod Holder

Fishing rods can be expensive; it is important that give your rods a good place to "rest" when they're not being used—a good place where they can hang securely, without any risk of getting any damage.

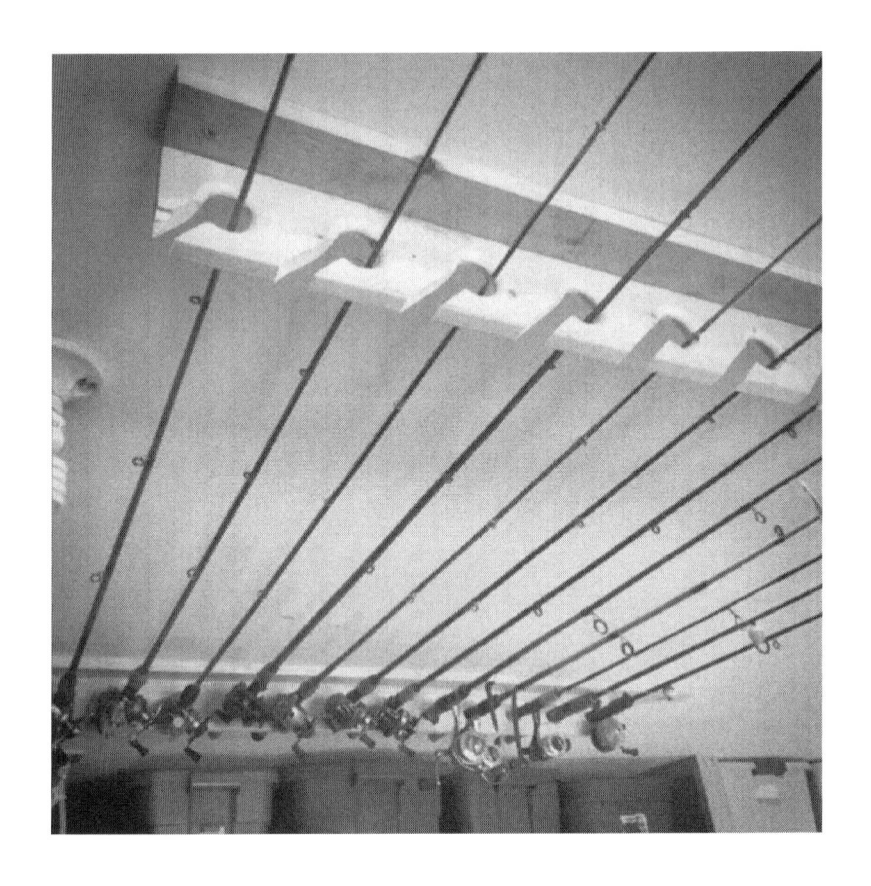

Supplies:
Wood
Wood saw
Wood carver
Sandpaper
Drill and screws
Hammer and nails
Varnish and brush (optional)

Instructions:

Gather all your fishing rods so you know how many slots you're going to prepare for the holder

Prepare the wood. You will need about four rectangular sheets of wood that are long enough for the lot that you have. Two of the sheets will be plain, they will be the base of the holder; and then the other two will have to be sculpted, so you can create small notches to hold the fishing rod at either end.

Attach the sculpted wood to the wooden base.

Run sandpaper through the entire surface to make it smooth. You may or may not apply varnish, depending on the esthetic you are trying to achieve.

Bolt the holder to the ceiling. Approximate the length of the fishing rod so you can position the front and back part of the holder to fit them perfectly in a straight line.

Arrange all your fishing rod.

Also, isn't this a lovely way to showcase your collection of fishing rods? If you are a proud fisherman, of course you would want to show off your equipment—and this is a really good way to do it.

Spray Paint Holder

If you use a lot of spray paint for the work you do in the garage, here's a simple thing you can for your cans so that they're not cluttered all over the place.

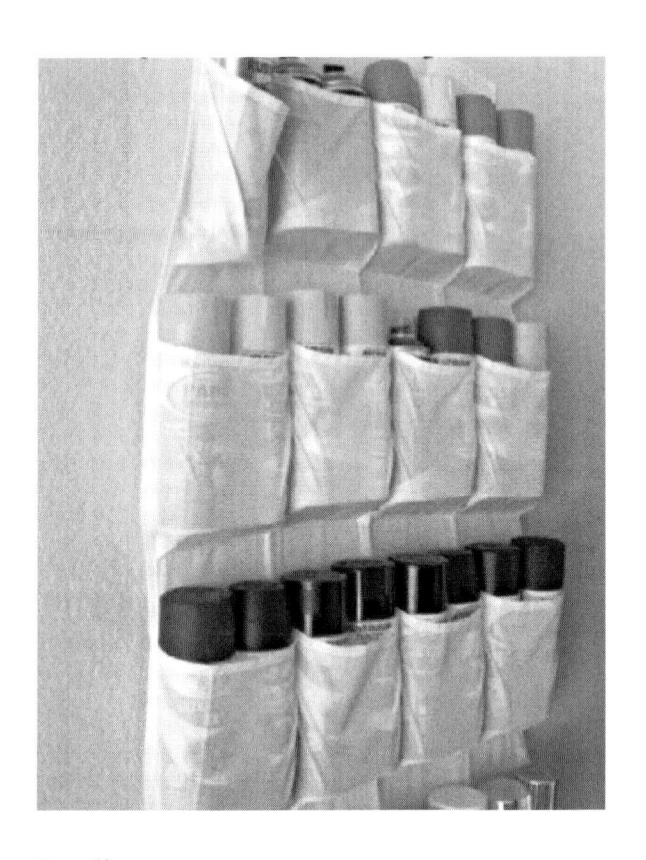

Supplies:
Plastic fabric
Thread and needle
Metal rings
Scissors

Instructions:
Obtain plastic fabric that's large enough. You can use an old shower curtain that you're no longer using.
Cut a large piece of the fabric to form the base of your pocket organizer; and cut small square or rectangular pieces of fabric to form the pockets or pouches.

Sew the pockets. You may do this by hand, but if you have a sewing machine, that may be a better idea.

Attach metal rings to the top, so you can hang the organizer on the wall.

Arrange your spray bottles into the pockets/pouches

You may design single or double pouches, depending on your aesthetic.

Bike and Scooter Stand

After a long day at work, it's nice to come home and relax. You come into the driveway, eager to go inside the house, but you realize it's just impossible for you to do that because there are bicycles and scooters littered in your garage. Well, how about assigning a parking space for the children's toys? The design is compact and quite practical; you can even put hooks for the helmet.

Supplies:
Wood
Wood saw
Sandpaper
Hammer and nails
Paint and brush
Hooks

Instructions:
Prepare the wood. You will need 6 large rectangular planks, 2 shorter rectangular planks, and several rectangular blocks to form the dividers. You will have to cut the edges of the rectangular blocks to give it a 45-degree slope.
Assemble the larger pieces of the design, to build the main frame.
Then attach the diagonally cut wood to form the barriers or division.
Make sure everything is secure.
Run sandpaper through surface and apply paint.
Attach 3-5 hooks at the topmost wooden plank. This is where you will put the helmets.
Arrange the bikes and scooters.

It is important that you're able to teach children to take responsibility of their toys, especially bikes and scooters. By assigning a specific place for these things, you teach them to be more disciplined—so they wouldn't just drop their bikes anywhere in the front house when they're done using it.

The Kid's Parking Lot

Here's another parking space idea for much bulkier toys.

Supplies:
Paint and brush
Masking tape

Instructions:
Determine the position of each toy car, bicycle, or scooter. Park them facing the wall, in the most convenient manner.
To be able to paint a straight line, you need to line two masking tapes on the floor, so you can paint the pavement, and simply take the tape off as soon as it's dry. This will leave a very clean line that's going look really nice.

Hanging Crate Case

Here's another idea you can use for crate storage.

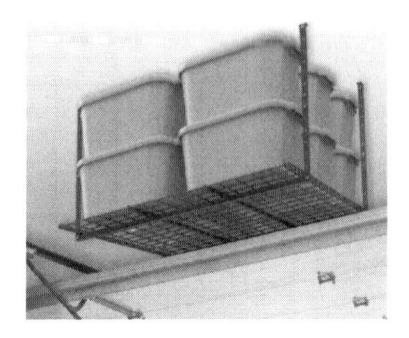

Supplies:
Metal lattice work
Metal strips
Drill and screw

Instructions:
You will need a metal mesh that's strong enough to carry the weight of the crates/boxes. You will also need a few pieces of metal strips/bars that will hold the base in place.
Assemble the hanging shelf by bolting four metal strips vertically, from the ceiling. Connect the two front strips/bars, horizontally, with one that is of a longer length; and do the same with the two pairs at the back.
Lay the metal mesh on top of the bolted metal strips/bars and screw it in place. Make sure the whole structure is secure.
Arrange the crates/box on the shelf.

Metal Pail Organizers

Supplies:
Metal pails
Black paint
Stencil

Instructions:
Gather all your small knick knacks and determine how many pails you'll need to be able to contain all of them.
To do the labels on the pails, you will need to prepare a stencil. You need to print your labels on a sheet of hard paper or plastic, cut out the

actual letters so you are left with just the background. Once you have the stencil, lay it on one side of the pail and run black paint over it Arrange all the things in their respective pails and arrange all the pails in the shelves.

If you have nails, screws, bolts, brackets and other carpentry or crafting materials, you can store them in pails so they won't look messy in your garage.

Covered Parking

Here's another parking idea for kids that will protect their toy vehicles from adverse weather conditions.

Supplies:
Plastic roof
PVC pipes
Adapters/sections
Thick cloth
Hole puncher
Shower curtain rings

Instructions:
Prepare the metal framework of the design. Are you going to have a square garage or a rectangular garage? Regardless of the design you will need several pipes and adapters that will connect the pieces together so you may build some sort of tent or structure. Assemble all the pieces together, making sure it is secure.

Prepare the curtains that will form the walls of the parking lot. Any tough fabric will do, such as plastic or cheesecloth. You will need to punch holes, so you can attach shower curtain rings to the curtains. Hang the curtains around the covered parking lot

Attach the plastic roof over the framework—making sure it is secure enough.

Paint Jars

If you do a lot of work in your garage and you have a lot of paint, you may want to get rid of the ugly paint cans. Instead of keeping the cans, you can choose to transfer the paint into mason jars, so they will look more esthetically appealing. Some shops also provide paint refills. By using jars, you lessen the waste that you regularly deal with and help save the environment, at the same time.

Supplies:
Mason jars
Paint
Labeler

Instructions:
Transfer the paint to the different jars
Label each jar accordingly, so you never confuse one color from the other, even if you already empty the jar
Arrange all the paint jars on the shelves.

Individual Locker

Before heading out of the house, you normally have a few things to grab—jacket, boots, or bag. When dealing with a large family, this can often be a messy affair. Have you seen my pink coat? Where is my favourite scarf? In school, children are able to keep their personal belongings in a locker—so why can't you do the same at home? Just like a normal locker, one space is assigned per person and the owner can decide what to put in his own space.

Supplies:
Wood
Wood saw
Sandpaper
Hammer and nails
Paint and brush
Cabinet handles
Hooks

Instructions:
Determine how many open lockers you need to make. That will depend on the number of people in your house.
Prepare the wood that you're going to use. For every locker, you will need to long rectangular sheets to form the sides of the locker, five shorter rectangular sheets to form the shelves, and four rectangular pieces of food to form the drawer at the bottom of the locker.
Assemble the drawer and attach the drawer handle.
Assemble the rest of the locker—positioning the different shelves according to your specific need. Make sure everything is secure.
Attach the hooks for the coats and other things.

Hanging Fish Rod Rack

Here's another idea for your precious fishing rods. This does not require much work because it only involves hanging metal racks high up to the ceiling, well away from all the other clutter in the storage and garage.

Supplies:
Metal racks
Drill and screws

Instructions

Obtain large metal racks. If you cannot find out you can have some made. They ought to be large enough to fit your entire collection. Bolt the racks to the ceiling. Make sure that it is secure enough to carry the weight of your entire collection. Make sure both racks are properly aligned so that you can hang the rods in a straight line. Arrange the rods on the rack. Handle them carefully as you do so, if you do not want them to break.

This design can accommodate a lot of fishing rods, so if you have a larger collection, this is going to be perfect.

Ball Bins

Supplies:
Electric drill
½ inch boring bit
Phillips head bit
Lumber: 4 pcs each - 1.5ft, 2.5ft, 4ft
Box of decking screws
14 pcs 36-inch bungee cords

Instructions:
Build one side of the frame by forming a rectangle with the 2.5foot and 4foot boards. Attach using 2 deck screws at each corner. Repeat on the second side.

On the inside corners of one of the rectangular frames, screw on 1.5-foot boards. Use two screws at each corner for this, then repeat with the other rectangular frame.

With your wood-boring bit, drill ½ inch holes across the top and at the bottom of this frame. Check to ensure that each hole has at least 6inches of space apart.

Stretch up the bungee cords from top to bottom and across the frame. Attach this bin to your garage wall with the use of 4-inch screws. Place your sports balls and secure them tight against the cords.

Ceiling Storage

Supplies:
Stud finder
Chop saw
Drill and screws
Tape measure
Dryer sheets
Wood glue
2x4s

Paintbrush
Plastic bins
Palm sander
Stain in desired finish

Instructions:
Measure the size of the bins and make sure you have enough clearance from the ceiling.
Create "I" shaped beams by laying one 2x4 flat and putting another 2x4 on its side and top with another flat 2x4. Use a drill and wood screws to attach these together.
Use a palm sander to smoothen rough edges and 220-grit paper plus a dryer sheet to clean off the surfaces.
Apply desired stain using a paintbrush and wipe excess off with a clean, dry cloth. Dry completely before installation.
Using a stud finder, locate the ceiling rafter and screw on the first beam in the middle. This will help support the weight of the bin.
Make a mark the same width as the bin and secure the second beam using the same process as the first beam. Slide these beams into place.
Slide in the plastic containers with the stored items. Label them outside for easy retrieval.

Hanging Storage Jars

Supplies:
Canning jars
Head screw driver
Hammer
6 screws
scrap piece of wood or a hard, flat surface
Flat-head nail

Instructions:
Separate the jar from their rims and flat top.
Position the flat top on the scrap piece of wood. You may use any flat surface to put a hole in. Hammer the nail into the centre of the flat top, just wide enough to make a small hole.
Place the flat top back inside the rim. Screw the entire lid on to the underside of a shelf or cabinet where you will hang the jars from.
Add the items you want to store inside the jars.
Pegboard Organizer

Supplies:
Pegboard panel
Measuring tape
Pencil
Circular saw or table saw
1x2x8 furring strips
1x2x8 trim
Paint
2" wood screws
Painting supplies
1/4 "finishing nails
Anchors
Hammer
Assorted peg hooks

Instructions:

Based on the size of your pegboard, determine the number of furring strips you will need. Make sure there is at least enough to make a frame under the board. For larger boards, add furring strips for the centre of the board spaced no more than 2 feet apart.

Measure the height of your board and cut two furring strips to that measurement minus 3 inches. You will need at least 2 pcs.

Make a line where the top of the pegboard should sit.

Place the vertical furring strips with the top edge against the level line. Use this level to ensure the furring strips are straight.

Secure these to the wall using 2" wood screws.

If no wall studs are available, use enough anchors for wall material that is not sturdy enough.

Add wood screws about every 6" apart from the frame and on the centre supports.

You can further customize the pegboard by painting it. Choose paint that has at least a bit of sheen to withstand scuffs and for it to clean.

There are a lot of pegboard accessories you can install (hooks, baskets, shelves, etc). It is up to you to organize what items make the most sense in your garage.

Angled PVC Storage Rack

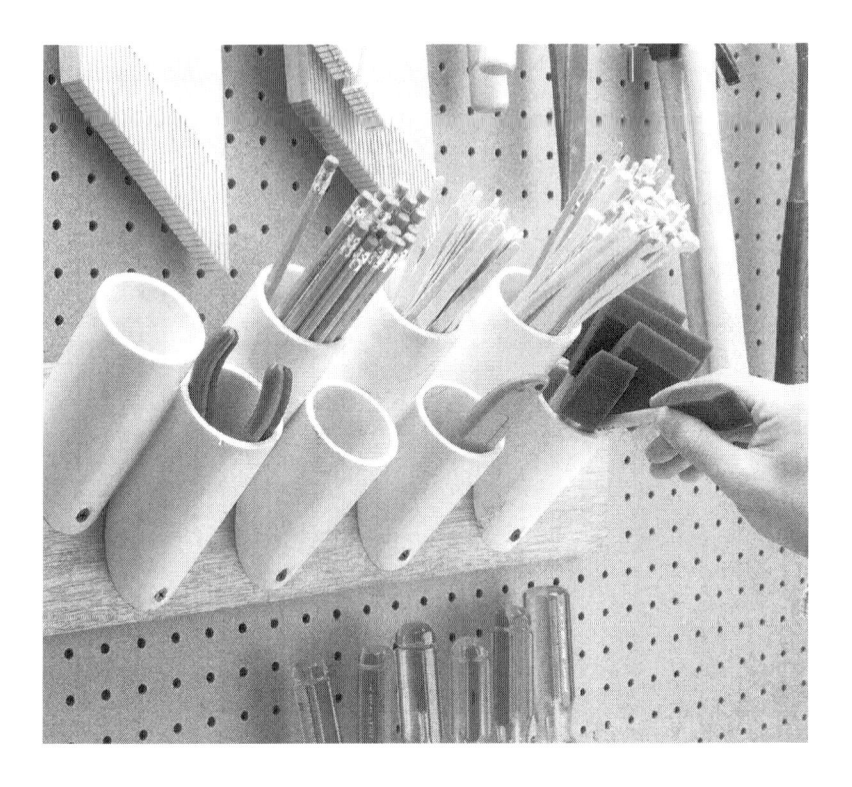

Supplies:
Sch. 40 PVC pipe 5inch length
Measuring tape
Pvc Pipe cutter
1pc 5/8" drywall screws
Drill with ¼" bit

Instructions:
Cut an angle on each pvc pipe and measure according to size desired. Drill the pipe using a drill and drywall screws to secure against the wall or board.

Once installed, you can display small objects or tools. Plan on which items go into which pipe according to the diameters.

Tape Dispenser

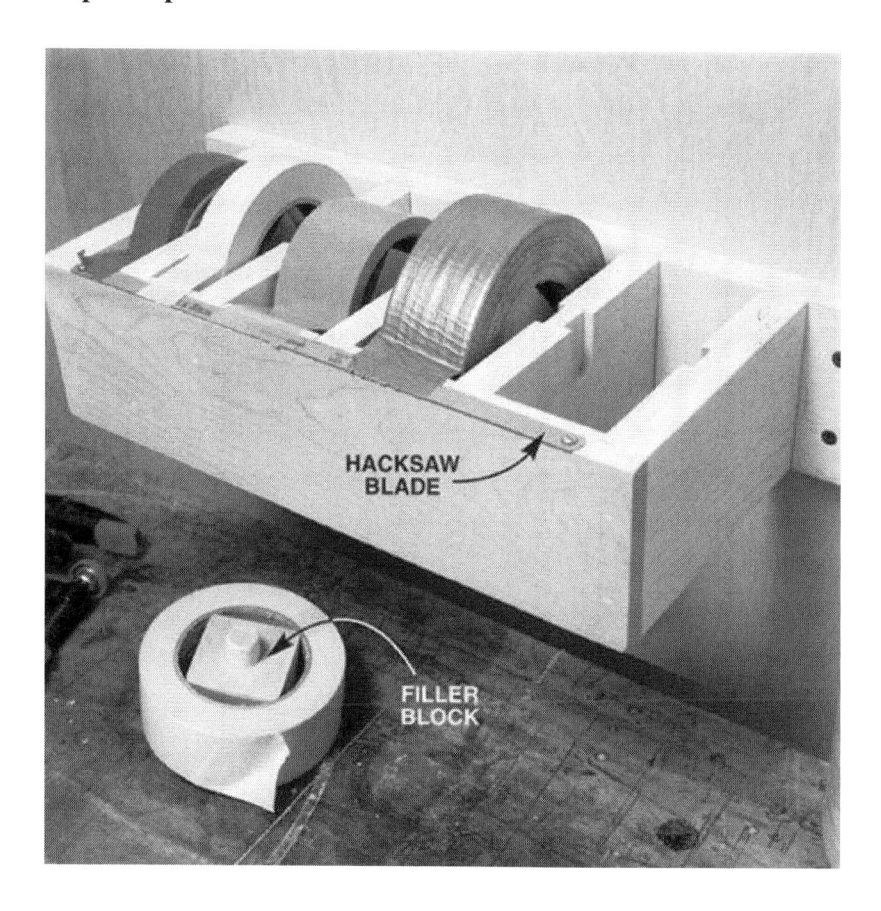

Supplies:
Scraps of lumber or plywood
Hacksaw blade
Screws

Instructions:

Make a filler block measuring 2-2/16-inch squares and round the corners until you get a tight fit inside the roll.

Fit an axle that measures ¾ inch dowel and place this slot into dividers.

Attach a hacksaw blade at the front panel to serve as the tape-cutting edge.

Arrange different kinds of tape in this dispenser. This will make the right tape more accessible when in need.

Screwdriver Coat Rack

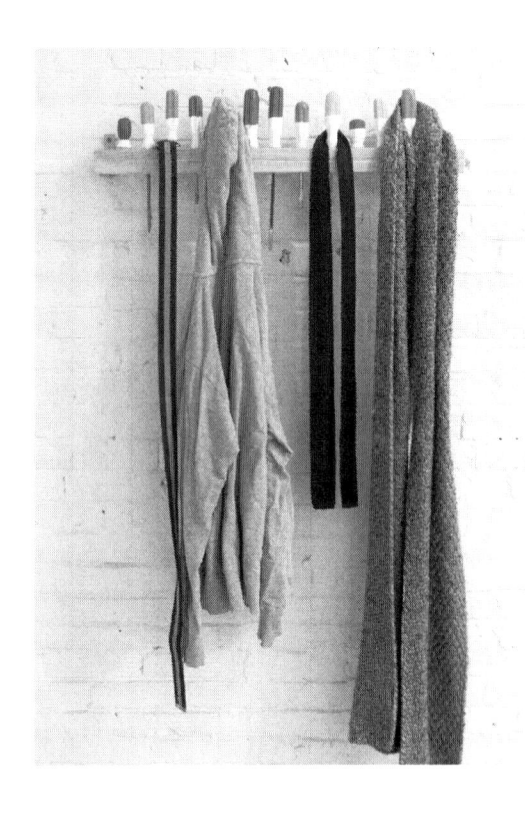

Supplies:
Old screwdrivers or hand tools
Plastic Dip (Multi Colour set)
Oak table leg
220 Grit Sandpaper
L-brackets
RYOBI 18-volt cordless drill with assorted drill bits

Instructions:
Clean off the dirt and grease from all your tools before assembly.
Dip to re-coat the screwdriver handles in Plastic Dip, first in white then in an assortment of colours.
Space out holes every 4 inches at least, giving enough area to hang coats.
Drill the holes on your board. Use 2 L-brackets for mounting.
To remove pencil marks, use a 220-grit sandpaper to sand the board.
Screw the L-brackets to the wall and the screw the oak leg to the L-brackets. This gives a strong and steady support.
Now your coat hanger is ready. You may also hang other pieces of clothing such as scarves or belts for easy access.

Chapter 10 - DIY Projects for Decluttering Your Home Office

Do you work from home and need to maintain a home office? Just like a work space in a genuine corporate environment it is supposed to be clean, organized, and functional. Clutter will get in the way and will affect your rate of productivity. It can easily mess with your brain and disrupt your functionality, so you need to keep your workspace in the home, as professional as possible.

There should be a definitive separation between the office space and the rest of the house, so that when you enter this room, you are forced to immediately transition to work-mode. And like most office spaces, especially the most corporate setting, you can achieve a professional image by applying these decluttering and organizational designs.

Cord Organizer

Supplies:
Box of Binder clips in various sizes
Your desktop surface

Instructions:
Clip the binder clips to the preferred edge of your desktop. Place these at the back of the desk to make use of the best orientation that can hide the wires.
Feed each of the charger cords through the largest side of the clip arm. Slip the cord head through the cord head sideways. If the cord is too large for this, remove the clip arm from the clip. Put the cord within the top clip arm, then reattach the clip arm.
Your desk is now less cluttered and free from tangles wires and cords.

Hanging Notepad

Supplies:
Pipe, dowel, or a long skinny branch
2pcs leather strips that are eat least 40" long
Thin leather cord
12"-24" roll of paper
Hammer
1" nails
1 clothespin

Instructions:
Cut the leather straps according to the measurement you want it to hang on the wall.

Determine the height of the roll of paper you need. Fold the first strip in half to form a loop, then hold the bottom of the loop at the desire height you want. Pinch the ends of the strips together above each other. Hammer a nail through the ends where they meet on the wall.

Slip your roll of paper through the branch, then slip one side of the branch into the first loop on the wall.

Fold the second strip to make a loop, and slide this loop under the other side of the branch.

While holding the branch at level height, hammer a nail into the folded strip to keep it in place.

You can then lengthen the paper roll according to your preference ad use it for your notes and memos.

The Case of the Router

The router is not exactly unappealing, but its shape is awkward and the wires and cords can be very annoying. It never goes with any décor you have and it destroys your aesthetic. The "case" is going to resolve this issue and it's hardly a DIY project.

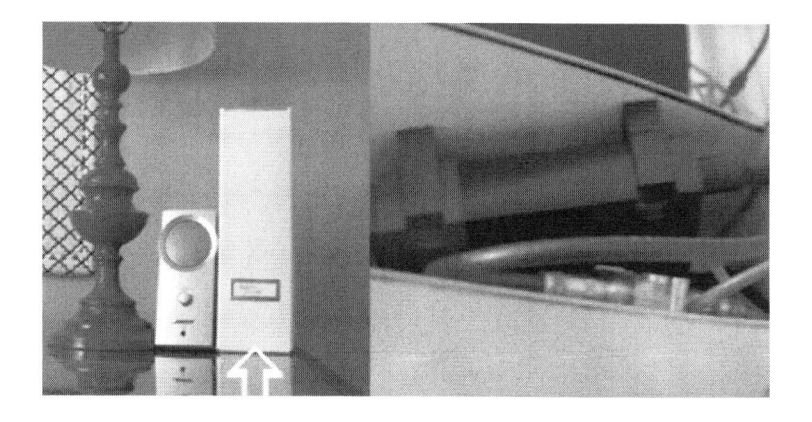

Supplies:
Desk organizer

Instructions:
Find a desk organizer or buy one if you don't have a used one lying around
Put the router into the desk organizer and squeeze in the wires and cords so that it does not show at all.

Now your router will look like a stack of files on the table. It's out of the way and it will just look as if you have

Fan Mail

Do you have a busted old electric fan that is on its way to the bin? Of course, you can decide to throw it away, but you're wasting a great opportunity to create the coolest storage equipment if you do.

Supplies:

Old broken-down desk fan (small)

Metal or wire cutter

Paint and brush (optional)

Instructions:

Clean your old broken-down electric fan, preferably a desk fan, and paint it a color that you want if you want spruce it up and add a bit more character to it.

Remove the "movable parts", such as the motor and its accessories, but leave the metal case.

Detach the front cover/case and cut the top half and attach it back to the fan. By cutting a part of the front, you will have a slot that's perfect enough to hold any of your incoming mail.

This, of course, is not an ideal design, but it turns your trash into something useful and it won't cost you anything but time, so it's such a cool idea. It gives a whole new meaning to the word, "fan mail", right?

Chapter 11 - Turning Method into Habit

Now that you have discovered ways on how to do your own de-cluttering, it is up to you to maintain your routine. Most of the time, de-cluttering feels like working out. It can be very challenging to get started. But once you get the ball rolling, you will have with a feeling of fulfillment and satisfaction. Capitalize on your small wins, and keep moving forward with this motivation in mind.

There will be days when you will feel down and un-motivated. When this happens, think about how it feels to have done de-cluttering. If it makes you feel good, then why not go ahead and do it? Remember why you started in the first place. Take photos of after de-cluttering and cleaning to compare the results. Remember the sense of peace and happiness as a result of a clutter-free home.

Celebrate your small wins until decluttering becomes muscle memory. Continue to work on it every single day, no matter how small your progress is. Each action gets you somewhere. And that is part of building up your habits to make de-cluttering a part of your daily life and not as a chore.

Conclusion

Living in today's world, it all becomes too easy to become a cluttered individual. Everything seems to go by at light speed. It becomes easy to be a cluttered individual. But with less clutter, there will be more room for you to do the things you love with the people you love. You will have the freedom of using the reclaimed space any way you want. You are not only making room in a physical sense, but you are, above all else, making room for clarity. A clear mind can give you better productivity and more joy and happiness. The chaos that once was there seems to drown out. And to think – all it takes is a few minutes of every day to clear out a small space. With a little faith and due diligence, you can live your life the best it can be.

-- Luigi Harbin

Dear Reader,

Thanks for exploring this book with me. Now that you know a handful of DIY decluttering projects…

…why not take one step further and declutter all aspects of your life?

You'll love the other book, because it complements this one.

Get it now.

Thanks,
Luigi

P.S. Reviews are like giving a warm hug to your favourite author. We love hugs.

https://www.amazon.com/dp/B07Q6BXH8N

Author Biography

Luigi Harbin is a lecturer who has a decade of experience…

… working in the Quality Management Industry.

He currently lives in Washington ... and is the successful author of the Declutter Workbook series.

When he isn't busy putting together presentation slides for classes of 40, he enjoys a spot of tidying up and organizing. It is this precise ritual that allows him to gather his thoughts freely and put some order into the chaos that is life.

Check Out Other Books

Declutter Workbook: A Step by Step Practical Guide to Organising Your Life
https://www.amazon.com/dp/B07GJBNGM3

Printed in Great Britain
by Amazon